In Praise
of
Apples

IN PRAISE
of
APPLES

A Harvest of History,
Horticulture
& Recipes

MARK ROSENSTEIN

Lark Books

Dedicated to the spirit of John Chapman—a real man, a real legend

Editor: Chris Rich
Art Direction: Dana Irwin
Production: Elaine Thompson
Photography: Evan Bracken

Library of Congress Cataloging-in-Publication Data
Rosenstein, Mark, 1952-
    In praise of apples : a harvest of history, horticulture & recipes /
by Mark Rosenstein.
       p.   cm.
    Includes index.
    ISBN 1-57990-124-7
    1. Cookery (Apples)   2. Apples.   I. Title.
   TX813.A6R67   1996
   641.6'41–dc20   96-22156
                               CIP

10 9 8 7 6 5 4 3 2 1

Published by Lark Books
50 College Street
Asheville, North Carolina, U.S.A. 28801

© 1996 by Mark Rosenstein

Distributed by Random House, Inc., in the United States, Canada,
    the United Kingdom, Europe, and Asia

Distributed in Australia by Capricorn Link (Australia) Pty Ltd.,
    P.O. Box 6651, Baulkham Hills Business Centre, NSW 2153, Australia

Distributed in New Zealand by Tandem Press Ltd., 2 Rugby Rd.,
    Birkenhead, Auckland, New Zealand

Printed in Hong Kong by Oceanic Graphic Printing

ISBN 1-57990-124-7

FRONT COVER: PHOTOGRAPH COURTESY OF
THE WASHINGTON STATE APPLE COMMISSION,
WENATCHEE, WA

TABLE OF CONTENTS

APPLE PICKING   ARTIST UNIDENTIFIED
NEW YORK STATE HISTORICAL ASSOCIATION, COOPERSTOWN, NY

INTRODUCTION

Three years ago, I stood on a street corner with my old friend and present publisher, Rob Pulleyn, discussing an idea for a book. What we imagined wasn't a cookbook. Even though

In Praise of Apples is about food, it isn't really a cookbook—it's an adventure—one that I had as I wrote it and one that I hope you'll have as you read and use it.

In creating culinary celebrations, I like to think I've touched other people's lives. I've certainly been interested in how food has shaped my own. In fact, food and drink have become my telescope and my microscope—the instruments I've used to understand this miracle and mystery we call our lives. Food has always carried me far beyond itself and the ways in which I prepare, serve, and eat it.

This book is one of blended flavors, with the apple at its center. When the adventure of writing it first started, I could only see separate pieces of the larger picture—a stem, a core, a seed. I discovered, for example, that cider could be used as a thickener in vegetable stocks. Every previous attempt I'd made to create a vegetable stock that wasn't too thin to reduce for use as a sauce had failed. Other discoveries followed, and now I see a story much greater than the scope of any single aspect of apples—or of any single life.

Apples are more than something to eat. For centuries, they've been intertwined in the myths, economics, culture, and developing technologies of countries throughout the world. At one time, this remarkable fruit played a central role in the daily routines of farms in Colonial America, England, and northern France. Apples have had an immense influence on thousands of lives.

I hope that as you read this book, you'll put it down to have your own adventures. Go to the kitchen and cook. Plant a small orchard. Meet people who bring some of the earth's bounty into their own lives; seek out apples, ciders, and vinegars to taste; make "frozen heart" applejack on the coldest night of the year—and, above all, share your adventures with someone else, in praise of apples.

Braeburn

Choosing
THE RIGHT APPLE

Criterion

Selecting Apples

If you've ever cut through the crust of a steaming apple pie, only to discover that the apples inside look like they should have been canned as applesauce, you'll understand one reason why *In Praise of Apples* starts off with this chart. Your grandmother may have known which apples hold their shape when they're baked and which turn into a purée, but as modern consumers, many of us aren't aware that each of the thousands of different apple varieties is best used in particular ways.

Chances are, you'll find only a limited number of these apples in your region, but by all means try the ones available. Extend your search beyond your grocery-store aisles, too. The four or five varieties that are probably stocked there—year after year after year—look good, keep well, and sometimes even taste good, but they represent only a tiny number of the tastes, textures, and aromas available in apples from around the world. Visit tailgate and farmers' markets, agricultural fairs, and your local orchardists; you're bound to find a few exceptional varieties.

DESSERT APPLE:	*the best kind to eat fresh*
SALAD APPLE:	*the least likely to discolor when peeled or cut*
COOKING APPLE:	*good for making both applesauce and purée*
SAUCE APPLE:	*cooks to a purée easily*
PIE APPLE:	*holds its shape when baked*
CIDER APPLE:	*makes good juice and cider*
VINTAGE APPLE:	*juice doesn't need to be blended with juice from other varieties*

Fuji

Gala

NAME	USE			KEEPER	DESCRIPTION
	DESSERT	COOKING	CIDER		
ARKANSAS BLACK	🍎	🍎 Pie		🍎	Medium-size; red to almost purple-red. Originated in Benton County, Arkansas around 1870, possibly as a seedling of the Winesap. Firm, fine grained, and moderately juicy
ASHMEAD'S KERNEL	🍎		🍎	🍎	Russet brown, with orange or bronze cheek. Famous English apple; originated in Gloucester around 1700 and is still widely grown. Reported to be a seedling of Nonpareil
ASHTON BROWN JERSEY			🍎 Vintage		Bittersweet, vintage variety found in Hereford orchards planted in the 1920s to 1930s. Produces high-quality juice and a full-bodied, medium-bittersweet cider
BALDWIN			🍎	🍎	Also known as Butters Apple, Woodpecker, and Felch. Widely grown in North America until the 1930s; replaced by McIntosh. High sugar levels
BRAEBURN	🍎	🍎 Pie			Crunchy, tangy-sweet, New Zealand apple discovered as a chance seedling in 1950
BRAMLEY'S SEEDLING		🍎 Sauce			The benchmark of high-acid cooking apples. Originated in Southwell, Nottinghamshire, England
BULMER'S NORMAN			🍎		Introduced from Normandy to England in the early 1900s. Produces sweet, astringent, fast-fermenting juice and mildly bittersweet cider
CALVILLE BLANC	🍎	🍎 Pie	🍎		The classic dessert apple of France; cultivated since the 1500s. May have originated in Germany. Can contain almost as much vitamin C as an orange
CHISEL JERSEY			🍎		English variety which produces bittersweet, astringent juice and a full-bittersweet cider. The term Jersey (pronounced "jay-see") denotes a bitter apple
CORTLAND	🍎 Salad	🍎 Sauce	🍎		A cross made in 1898 between McIntosh and Ben Davis. Flavor between sweet and acid; fruit very juicy

Royal Gala

Golden Delicious

NAME	USE			KEEPER	DESCRIPTION
	DESSERT	COOKING	CIDER		
COX'S ORANGE PIPPIN	🍎	🍎 Pie	🍎	🍎	Classic English apple. Raised in the early 1800s from a seed of Ribston Pippin. Pear-like aroma when baked. High in vitamin C and parent of many prized varieties
EMPIRE	🍎	🍎	🍎	🍎	Cross between Red Delicious and McIntosh, introduced in 1966. White, crisp, juicy, sweet flesh
ESOPUS SPITZENBURG	🍎	🍎		🍎	A favorite of Thomas Jefferson's. Originated in Esopus, Ulster County, New York in the late 1700s. Likely parent of Jonathan; classified in the Baldwin apple family. Firm, crisp flesh
FOXWHELP			🍎 Vintage		Bittersharp, vintage English apple; dates back to the 1600s. Produces aromatic, musky-flavored cider
FUJI		🍎 Sauce		🍎	1939 cross between North American parents (Ralls Janet and Red Delicious), made on Japanese soil. Popular in Japan, China, and the U.S.
GALA	🍎			🍎	New Zealand cross between Cox's Orange Pippin and Golden Delicious. Small, with rich, honeyed flavor. Very juicy; dries well
GOLDEN DELICIOUS	🍎	🍎	🍎		Unrelated to Red Delicious. Originated as chance seedling in 1912 in Clay County, West Virginia. Crisp, juicy flesh. Second most popular dessert apple in the U.S.
GOLDEN RUSSET	🍎	🍎	🍎		Sweet, early North American variety dating back to the 1800s. Yellow, crisp, fine-textured flesh. Dries well
GRANNY SMITH	🍎	🍎	🍎		One of the first green apples in North America. Chance seedling grown in New South Wales, Australia; fruited in 1868
GRAVENSTEIN	🍎	🍎	🍎		Believed to have originated in Russia or Italy. Thin-skinned, juicy, and sweet as well as tart. A good summer apple that does not keep well

Granny Smith

Jonagold

NAME	DESSERT	COOKING	CIDER	KEEPER	DESCRIPTION
		USE			
GRIMES GOLDEN		🍎 *Sauce*	🍎	🍎	Originated near Fowlersville, West Virginia, close to the original nursery of Johnny Appleseed; may be one of his seedlings. Believed to be the parent of Golden Delicious. Very high sugar content
HYSLOP CRAB		🍎	🍎		A crab apple of unknown origins; first noted in 1869. Too astringent to be eaten fresh, but excellent for jelly, cider blending, and pickling. Also a good landscape tree. Fruit dries out very quickly, so use immediately
IDARED		🍎 *Pie*			Introduced in 1942 in Idaho. Highly aromatic. Skins are thick; flesh is juicy and slightly tart. Best used soon after harvest
JONAGOLD	🍎	🍎			Released by New York State's Geneva Station in 1968. Not well known in the U.S., but may be the world's favorite apple. Cross between Jonathan and Golden Delicious. Sweet-tart flesh
JONATHAN	🍎	🍎 *Pie*	🍎		Introduced in the 1820s; related to Esopus Spitzenburg. Best-selling U.S. apple during early part of this century. Does not keep well
LADY	🍎			🍎	Also known as Pomme d'Api. Has been culti-vated in France for over 300 years. Small and colorful; tender, crisp, and juicy flesh
MCINTOSH	🍎	🍎 *Sauce*	🍎		Discovered in 1796 near Dundela, Dundas County, Ontario, Canada. Introduced and named in 1870; important commercially only after the early 1900s. Now planted in most of the cold apple-growing regions of the world. Highly aromatic and spicy. Does not keep well
MICHELIN			🍎		Raised in Normandy; introduced to the U.S. in 1872. A medium-bittersweet, similar to Bulmer's Norman. Produces a sweet, mildly astringent juice and medium-bittersweet cider
MUTSU	🍎	🍎 *Sauce*	🍎	🍎	Also known as Crispin. Very sweet Japanese cross between Golden Delicious and Indo. Developed in the 1930s and introduced in the late 1940s. Known in Japan as the "Million Dollar Apple" for the high price it fetches

Newtown Pippin

Red Delicious

NAME	USE			KEEPER	DESCRIPTION
	DESSERT	COOKING	CIDER		
NEWTOWN PIPPIN	🍎	🍎	🍎	🍎	Famous Virginia apple—George Washington's favorite—also known as Albemarle Pippin, Mountain Pippin, Yellow Pippin, and Pippin. The oldest commercially grown, native variety in the U.S. First noted in 1759 in Newtown, Long Island. Crisp, tender, sweet-tart flesh. Not a salad apple, as it browns quickly
NONPAREIL	🍎		🍎 *Vintage*		Dates back to the 1500s. Probably originated in France; introduced to England during the reign of Queen Elizabeth I. Sweet-tart flesh. Makes an excellent cider by itself
NORTHERN SPY		🍎 *Pie*	🍎	🍎	May originally have been called Northern Pie. Very popular variety in the early 1900s. Juicy flesh; high in vitamin C. Medium to high acid content; often blended with crab apples or wild crabs to make cider. Newly planted trees don't produce fruit for several years.
NORTHWESTERN GREENING		🍎		🍎	A popular yellow apple in the northern U.S. Flesh is firm, tart, and juicy; skin is tough
PITMASTON PINEAPPLE	🍎				An old variety of russeted English dessert apple. Very small and very sweet. Flavor sometimes compared to that of pineapples
RED DELICIOUS	🍎				A chance seedling discovered in 1872 in Peru, Iowa; now the most popular apple in the U.S. Over 300 varieties available
RHODE ISLAND GREENING	🍎	🍎 *Pie*		🍎	A green apple, which dates back to the 1600s. One of the best pie apples in existence. Tart, greenish flesh also dries well
ROME BEAUTY		🍎	🍎		Discovered as a shoot sprouting from below the graft line of a tree in Rome Township, Ohio, in the 1820s. Crisp, tart flesh, and very thick skin
ROXBURY RUSSET	🍎	🍎	🍎	🍎	Probably the oldest named variety in North America; discovered in Roxbury, Massachusetts during the early seventeenth century. Very high sugar content. The medium-acid fruit produces a fine, clear cider with an aromatic flavor and a 6% alcohol content.

Rome Beauty

Winesap

NAME	DESSERT	COOKING	CIDER	KEEPER	DESCRIPTION
SMITH'S CIDER			🍎		Reported in 1817 in Bucks County, Pennsylvania; still under cultivation today
SPARTAN	🍎			🍎	Developed in 1936 in Summerland, British Columbia. Very flavorful, firm white flesh. A fairly disease-resistant cross between McIntosh and Newtown Pippin
STAYMAN WINESAP		🍎	🍎	🍎	A seedling of Winesap, raised in 1866 in Leavenworth, Kansas. Juicy, firm flesh. At one time, a major commercial apple, particularly in the eastern United States
SWAAR	🍎			🍎	Originated with Dutch settlers in the Hudson River Valley region of New York. Dates back to around 1770. High sugar content. Improves in flavor with storage. The apples hang on the tree for a long time and make a wonderful gift for wildlife.
SWEET COPPIN			🍎 *Vintage*		Typical of the Devon low-tannin cider apple. A pure, sweet, vintage variety; produces a sweet juice with no astringency and a sweet to mildly bittersweet cider
VIRGINIA (OR HEWE'S) CRAB			🍎		Thomas Jefferson favored this native North American crab apple. Trees requires little maintenance. Juice ferments very slowly to produce a highly flavored, dry cider
WINESAP	🍎	🍎	🍎		First described in 1804 in Philadelphia. An important apple in the cider industry of New Jersey. Very juicy flesh; vinous and strongly sweet-and-sour flavor. Best blended in cider with bland, sweet varieties
YARLINGTON MILL			🍎 *Vintage*		Vintage English apple, known for its high yields. Produces a sweet, slightly astringent juice and a medium-bittersweet cider
YORK IMPERIAL		🍎		🍎	Originated near York, Pennsylvania. Named also for its "imperial" keeping qualities

THE RECIPES

Before you dash off to the kitchen, take a good look at the tips in this section. They're designed to make the recipes easier to follow—and cooking with apples more fun. Whenever you're about to use a new recipe, read through it carefully first, make a shopping list, and check to see that you have all the necessary utensils, equipment, and supplies.

RECIPE HEADINGS

BASIC RECIPE INCLUDED: When you see this heading, you'll know that the recipe you're reading incorporates one or more of my "basic" recipes—recipes that I include within others. One, for example, is an Apple and Leek Stock that finds its way into many of the dishes I prepare. Rather than repeat instructions for making the stock every time it's called for, I've placed this recipe—and a few other basic recipes—in a single section (see pages 132–135).

Periodically, I make large batches of the Apple and Leek Stock. By reducing it, freezing it in ice-cube trays, and storing the cubes in sealed plastic bags, all I have to do when a recipe calls for stock is grab as many frozen cubes as I need.

ADDITIONAL RECIPE INCLUDED: When a particular dish goes exceptionally well with another, I've listed the complementary recipe under this heading. In the Turkey Roulade recipe on pages 58–59, for example, you'll find Apple Ratatouille (pages 82–83) listed as an "Additional Recipe." The roulade and ratatouille make a delicious combination.

HAVE ON HAND: There's nothing more upsetting than starting to prepare a dish, only to discover that you don't have the required equipment or utensils to complete it. Under this heading, I've listed the items that the average kitchen sometimes lacks—items such as charcoal smokers and meat grinders. If you don't have what you need, feel free to improvise or borrow from a friend.

INGREDIENTS: The ingredients for these recipes are listed in order of their use. Don't be surprised if, as you browse through a list, you find an ingredient listed twice. If apples are used twice in a given recipe, they may be listed twice, too.

It pays to keep an eye on your supplies of favorite ingredients, whatever these may be. If you've spent much time browsing through the recipes in this book, you'll understand why my own kitchen is rarely without fresh herbs—tarragon and basil in the summer, chives in the spring, and thyme and sage year round.

Notes: When these special tips are included, they often come at the end of the recipe, but be sure to read them before you shop for ingredients or start cooking.

BASIC KITCHEN EQUIPMENT

Excellent chefs, like fine mechanics, know that a good assortment of high-quality "tools" goes a long way toward guaranteeing success. You don't need hundreds of expensive items in order to make the dishes in this book, but you will need some basic utensils and equipment. Following is a list of these items:

Blender or food processor

Grater (hand)

Mixing bowls

Ovenproof casserole dishes

Racks for draining and cooling

Roasting pan with lid and rack

Sauté pans

Sheet pans

Skillets

Spatulas (rubber and metal)

Stirring spoon (wooden)

Stockpot

Wire whisk

SHOPPING FOR KITCHEN EQUIPMENT: Cooking should be fun, but it isn't when you're working with tools that aren't up to the job. When you purchase utensils, remember that well-made ones will outlive you. I've actually had chefs apply for work at my restaurant because they know that my collection of iron skillets has been in service for 25 years.

Heavy skillets and sauté pans will conduct heat better and last longer than lightweight equipment. Cast-iron skillets are best for sauté work and for very slow cooking. Although cast iron takes longer than other metals to heat up, it holds heat much better. The disadvantages of cast iron are that it can be hard to handle and will rust if it isn't thoroughly dried after each use.

Lined copper pans were once the choice of the professional French chef, but although copper is a wonderful heat conductor, the tin coating on these pans does wear out; exposure to the copper then discolors and even taints the food. A modern compromise is the copper pan lined with stainless steel. Although these pans are expensive, they'll last a lifetime or longer. Aluminum coated with stainless steel also works well; the aluminum serves as the heat conductor, and the stainless steel provides a non-reactive surface.

Apple-Cooking TIPS

HANDLING APPLES

When a recipe calls for unpeeled apples, always wash the apples well before using them.

Peeled, sliced, or cut apples quickly discolor. To prevent this, place the cut apples in a solution of 1 tablespoon lemon juice in 1/2 gallon (1.9 l) of water.

Refrigerate apples away from strong-tasting foods such as onions, and place them in perforated plastic bags to help retain their moisture.

SUBSTITUTIONS

Fresh apple juice and apple cider may be interchanged except when making or using cider reductions (see page 132).

COOKING EQUIVALENTS

1 POUND (454 G) APPLES	= *4 small, 3 medium, or 2 large apples*
	= *4 cups chopped or sliced apple*
	= *1-1/2 cups applesauce*
1 LARGE APPLE	
3-3/4" (9.5 CM) DIAMETER	= *2 cups sliced apple*
	= *1-1/4 cups grated apple*
	= *1-1/2 cups finely chopped apple*
	= *3/4 cup applesauce*
1 MEDIUM APPLE	
2-3/4" (7 CM) DIAMETER	= *1-1/3 cups sliced apple*
	= *3/4 cup grated apple*
	= *1 cup finely chopped apple*
	= *1/2 cup applesauce*
1 SMALL APPLE	
2-1/4" (5.7 CM) DIAMETER	= *3/4 cup sliced apple*
	= *1/2 cup grated apple*
	= *3/4 cup finely chopped apple*
	= *1/3 cup applesauce*
1 BUSHEL APPLES	= *4 pecks = 45 pounds = 20.4 kg*

MAKING PIES

2 to 2-1/2 pounds (.9 to 1.1 kg) of apples will suffice for a 9" or 10" (22.9 or 25.4 cm) pie. Use 4 to 5 large, 6 to 7 medium, or 8 to 9 small apples.

Considering the fact that cutting is a major part of cooking, an investment in three or four high-quality knives makes a lot of sense. In my "tool kit" are four knives, all with stainless steel blades.

Large chef's knife with 10"-long (25.4 cm) blade

Paring knife with 3"-long (7.6 cm) blade

Boning knife with thin, 7"-long (17.8 cm) blade

Slicing knife with 13"-long (33 cm) blade

Carbon steel blades are easier to sharpen, but unlike stainless steel blades, they discolor some foods.

Before purchasing a knife, test it for balance by holding it in your hand. People with smaller or larger hands than mine may find they're more comfortable with blades about 1" (2.5 cm) shorter or longer than mine. Also check to see that the visible portion of the blade and its hidden tang (the portion that extends into the handle) are a single, solid piece. The tang should extend all the way to the end of the handle.

For two reasons, I prefer knives with handles heavier than their blades. First, heavier handles feel better to me. More importantly, when you drop a knife with a heavy handle, the handle hits the floor first, preventing damage to the blade.

Have you ever wondered why it's easier to cut yourself with a dull knife than with a sharp one? Think about how much more effort it takes to cut with a dull knife and how much more likely you are to slip while exerting that kind of pressure. To keep my knives sharp, I use two different grits of emery cloth, a medium (or 80 grit) and a fine (or 220 grit). Hold the blade almost flat against the paper, and use a circular or slicing motion to sharpen the blade all the way to the handle.

To clean your knives, wash them with a little dish soap or—less frequently—with some scouring powder. Rinse and dry. Don't use a dishwasher, as the higher heat of the water in it can cause the metal to soften or lose its temper.

USING ELECTRIC STOVES

When I was younger, I prepared a lot of "split-second" dishes, racing with time over a responsive gas stove. Although I still prefer gas stoves, I now tend to use lower temperatures, cooking food slower and longer. (In retrospect, I sometimes wonder whether my youthful, frantic culinary displays weren't driven more by hormones than by a desire for great cuisine!)

The flames of a gas stove do provide valuable visual cues, and gas stove temperatures can be adjusted much more quickly than those of an electric stove. By using the tips that follow, however, you can tame an electric stove to do your bidding.

■ Avoid the "high" setting on an electric stove, except for rapid boiling of water or when using a wok. When high heat is called for in one of my recipes, preheat your pan over medium-high (8 or 9) heat instead.

■ When you lower the temperature, slide the pan off to the edge of the burner for a few moments. When the burner has lost its heat, slide the pan back onto it.

■ Learn to judge the intensity of your stove by holding your hand over (never on) the top of the burner.

COOKING TIMES

As a rule of thumb, the larger the cut of meat, fish, or vegetable, the lower the heat and the longer the time required to cook it. Conversely, the smaller the cut, the higher the heat and the shorter the cooking time. Oriental methods of cooking offer a great example. A wok is designed for rapid cooking over very high heat, and, as you know, Oriental cuisine requires very precise cutting and very small cuts. In Europe, where vast forests and deep coal mines provided ample fuel, long slow cooking of great sides of meat was the rule—and is a tradition we still favor.

This same rule of thumb applies when you're using a charcoal grill. To cook small steaks, use intense heat; for larger cuts, such as a leg of lamb, a low, slow fire is best.

CULINARY GLOSSARY

I've tried not to use cooking terms that are alien to most cooks, but if you find a term you're not familiar with, just flip to the glossary of cooking terms on pages 173–174.

The International Apple Institute, located in McLean, Virginia, recently treated the public to an important analysis of one critical aspect of apples—the various munching styles of apple eaters. Reprinted here are the Institute's expertly developed apple-eating profiles. Compare your own munching method with these descriptions.

THE COMPULSIVE WEDGER: Can't eat the apple whole. Must have perfect core-free wedges arranged neatly on a plate. Each wedge must equal one-eighth of an apple.

THE SPLITTER: Hates to deal with the core, but is not compulsive enough to bother with wedges. Chops the apple in half, removes the core, and munches contentedly. Muscle-bound types show off their brute force by twisting the apple in half with their bare hands (actually not very difficult to do).

THE CIRCLE STICKLER: A rebellious sort who slices the apple against the grain (across the core) to make round slices. He or she can often be found with convenient slices of cheese close at hand and uses the apple slices as if they were crackers.

THE TOP-TO-BOTTOM TYPE: A methodical muncher, he or she starts at the stem and munches all the way to the bottom without changing the apple's position until one vertical top-to-bottom pass has been completed. The apple is then rotated, and the muncher continues in the next lane until the whole piece of fruit is gone.

THE EQUATOR EATER: The muncher takes bites out of the center of the apple, all the way around, until the apple looks something like a mushroom on a mirror. He or she then attacks the top, and finally eats the bottom. This munching style is somewhat less convenient than others, as it leaves the muncher without a juice-free apple area to grip as he or she takes the final bites.

THE STREAKER: This eater prefers nude apples and does not care about the vitamins and fiber in apple skins, which are peeled right off, usually in one piece. The muncher then eats the apple either whole or sliced. The latter method is usually employed, as the apple's skinless state can lead to copious juice drippings.

THE CORE-FREE CRUNCHER: This type comes in two varieties. Type A loves gadgets and small appliances, and eats a lot of apples because doing so permits the use of apple-corers. Type B is a seedophobic and doesn't care what is necessary—a gadget, knife, or sharp fingernails—as long as every single seed can be removed before a bite of fruit is taken.

THE STEM PLUCKER: Before taking the first bite, this type grabs the stem and twists the apple, voicing one letter of the alphabet with each turn. The letter at which the stem comes off bears profound meaning, usually construed to be the first initial of a future spouse. (Married individuals take note: Turns can be modified to ensure that the stem comes out at the desired letter.) Especially curious Stem-Pluckers continue the ritual by poking the outside of the apple with the stem in order to determine the number of children they will have, which is said to be the number of attempts it takes to break the skin of the apple. In a recent, incredibly unscientific poll, three out of four people surveyed admitted to being Stem-Pluckers.

THE BLISSFUL GOURMAND: A member of this group is represented in the photo below. While deceptively polite, this muncher cares only to savor as much delicious apple flesh as is possible in the shortest period of time. Unhampered by compulsions regarding seeds, skins, or eating styles, the Blissful Gourmand is shamelessly addicted to the succulent flavor of fresh apples.

APPLE, BANANA, and STRAWBERRY FROTH

Whether you're celebrating the morning sunrise by sharing this drink with someone special, or treating yourself to a single serving, this recipe is as easy to prepare as it is enjoyable.

Yields
2 SERVINGS

INGREDIENTS

1 very ripe banana, peeled

1 medium-tart apple, peeled and cut into cubes

4 strawberries, capped

1/2 vanilla bean, split

1/2 cup (118 ml) fresh apple cider or sparkling cider

2 tablespoons honey

1/8 teaspoon cardamom

1 whole strawberry, split in half

METHOD

■ Place the banana, cubed apple, and strawberries in a blender. Scrape the inside of the vanilla bean into the blender, too. Add the honey and cardamom, and purée at high speed, gradually adding the cider at the same time.

■ Pour into a favorite set of glasses, garnish the glasses with the split strawberries, put up your feet, and enjoy.

MULLED CIDER

Apple cider is a marvelous beverage and can be used to make drinks ranging from a light Tisane de Pommes to a stronger Stone Fence Punch (see pages 22 and 23). This variation makes a wonderful fall or winter afternoon refresher.

Yields
5 CUPS (1.1 L)

INGREDIENTS

4 cups (.9 l) fresh apple cider

1/3 cup (40 g) light brown sugar,
tightly packed

1 cinnamon stick

4 whole cloves

1 star anise

1/2 teaspoon peeled, sliced, fresh ginger

1 stalk lemon grass, sliced
(or 1 sliced lemon)

1/2 bay leaf

Note: Lemon grass, a key ingredient in Thai cuisine, can be found in Asian food shops. To grow your own, set one or two stalks in water to root, and then plant in a large clay pot. Lemon grass will winter-kill, so keep the pot indoors during the cold months of the year.

METHOD

■ Combine all the ingredients in a saucepan. Place over medium heat, and stir until the sugar has dissolved. Bring to a boil, reduce the heat, and simmer, covered, for 10 minutes. Strain and serve.

TISANE *de* POMMES

A tisane is a light infusion that serves as an aid to digestion. Its name is derived from the Greek word *ptisane*, which means barely water, and indeed, the tisane of Hippocrates' times was barely water. In more recent times, the use of tisanes has been popularized by Michel Guerard at his spa in Eugenie-les-Bain, which he opened in 1972.

Yields

6 FIVE-OUNCE (148 ML) SERVINGS

HAVE ON HAND

1-quart (.9 l) glass jar

INGREDIENTS

2 large, tart apples

1/4 cup (40 g) raisins

1 tablespoon granulated sugar

2 whole coriander seeds

1/2 teaspoon whole cardamom seeds

1 teaspoon fresh ginger, peeled and sliced

4 cups (.9 l) water

METHOD

■ Preheat the oven to 350°F (177°C). Bake the whole, unpeeled apples for about 45 minutes or until they are wrinkled. Cut into quarters, place in the glass jar, and add the remaining ingredients. Cover with boiling water, and let the ingredients steep for 1 to 2 hours. Strain into glasses, and drink warm.

STONE FENCE PUNCH

A better name for this concoction might be "Punched by a Stone Fence." The beverage was a favorite among farm workers at the turn of the nineteenth century and could very well have contributed to the decline of the American farm. A glass or two definitely reduces one's desire to work. I offer this recipe knowing that my readers are of a more sensible and disciplined nature than their farming ancestors.

Yields
3 QUARTS (2.8 L)

HAVE ON HAND

1-gallon (3.8 l) glass jar

1-gallon (3.8 l) jug with tight seal

INGREDIENTS

2 cups (473 ml) Calvados (apple brandy)

2 cups (473 ml) dark rum

8 cups (1.9 l) fresh apple cider

1 orange, sliced

1/2 lemon, sliced

2 cinnamon sticks

10 whole cloves

METHOD

■ Combine all the ingredients in a large glass jar, and set aside for 3 days. Strain and store in a tightly sealed jug. Serve without mixers, either "neat" or over ice.

Apple WASSAILING

Apple wassailing, a form of which is still practiced in some rural areas of England on Twelfth Night, is an ancient ritual in which the apple is celebrated as a symbol of fertility. Some English men and women, in fact, still believe that wassailing is their best assurance of a successful apple crop.

In older forms of this ritual, villagers gathered beneath the largest tree in the orchard and suspended pieces of cider-soaked toast from its branches. The toast, it was thought, would attract robins, once believed to be good spirits. To prevent evil spirits from wending their way to the huge apple tree, strategically placed villagers fired shotguns into the air throughout the orchard.

Singing participants would dance around the tree, dousing its trunk and roots with hard cider and quenching their own thirst as well. As time passed, the wassailing ceremony—heretofore a solemn tribute to the deity of the apple tree—took on an extraordinarily jolly tone, possibly due to the quantity of cider consumed.

Wassail, made from cider and ale, is still a traditional English drink and is frequently consumed on Twelfth Night and Christmas Eve. It is usually served in a bowl, with roasted apples floating on its surface.

POMMES à L'EAU-de-VIE

This very old recipe traditionally calls for the small and beautiful Lady apple, one of the oldest varieties known. Some pomologists claim that this apple is the same one found in the ancient Forest of Api, in France. Whether it is or not, the brightly flushed Lady apple remains crisp, sweet, and delicious until spring and is often used as a decorative fruit during the holiday season.

Yields
1 QUART (.9 L)

2-quart (1.9 l) saucepan

*Wide-mouthed jar large enough
to hold the apples*

INGREDIENTS

6 very small dessert apples

2-1/2 cups (500 g) sugar

2 cups (473 ml) water

1 teaspoon cloves

1 teaspoon cinnamon

*A fifth (.8 l) of brandy or Calvados
(apple brandy)*

■ You'll start by making an apple-flavored simple syrup. Fill a 2-quart (1.9 l) saucepan halfway with water. Bring to a boil over high heat. Drop in the whole, unpeeled apples, and boil for 3 minutes. Drain well, and wipe dry with a clean towel.

■ In a 2-quart (1.9 l) saucepan, bring the sugar and water to a boil. Using a needle or fork, prick each apple all over. Drop the apples into the boiling syrup, reduce the heat, and simmer for 15 minutes.

■ Remove the pan from the heat. When the apples have cooled, remove them from the syrup, and place them in a wide-mouthed jar. Add the cloves and cinnamon to the simple syrup, and bring it to a boil again. Pour 1/2 cup of the boiling syrup over the apples. (Reserve the rest of the syrup; it makes a fine substitute for the syrup called for in the Cider Lemon Sorbet recipe on pages 112–113.)

■ When the jar's contents are cool, fill the remainder of the jar with brandy or Calvados, and allow the contents to sit for a few days to develop the flavor. Serve in glasses with chunks of flavored apples from the jar.

Frozen Heart APPLEJACK

If you've ever been tempted to try your hand at distilling, but you haven't because owning a still is against the law, a hard winter will provide you with the opportunity to try. This centuries-old, no-tech method is incredibly easy and produces a truly potent beverage. You'll need 1 gallon (3.8 l) of dry, hard cider, two open-topped jugs, two bone-chilling winter nights, and an ice pick.

Fill one jug with cider to within a few inches of the top, and set it outside to freeze hard overnight. In the morning, before daylight, heat the ice pick, and use it to punch a hole down through the frozen cider. Pour the thick, liquid center into the second jug, and reserve. Discard what remains in the first jug.

On the next cold night, repeat the process, leaving the second jug and its contents outdoors to freeze. Drain off the unfrozen liquid in the morning. If the thermometer registered -5°F (-21°C) each night, the applejack that you drain from the second jug is likely to have a 13% alcohol content. If the temperatures dropped as low as -30°F (-34°C), your applejack may have an alcohol content as high as 33%—a 66-proof beverage guaranteed to make you feel warm no matter how low temperatures drop.

APPLE BREAD *with* WALNUT APPLE BUTTER

This simple but delicious bread and the luscious butter that accompanies it make a wonderful breakfast treat but can be served with any meal or enjoyed as a hearty snack.

Yields

12 THICK SLICES

BASIC RECIPE INCLUDED

Apple Cider Reduction
(PAGE 132)

HAVE ON HAND

6-cup (1.4 l) loaf pan

Mixer with paddle blade

BREAD INGREDIENTS

2 medium cooking apples, peeled and cored

3 cups (360 g) whole wheat flour

3 whole cloves, ground

3 whole allspice seeds, ground

1 teaspoon salt

2 tablespoons yeast

1 cup (237 ml) warm water

1 tablespoon butter, melted

BUTTER INGREDIENTS

1/2 cup (60 g) toasted walnut meal (see "Note")

1 cup (230 g) unsalted butter, softened

3 tablespoons Apple Cider Reduction

1/2 teaspoon nutmeg

1/2 teaspoon allspice

1/2 teaspoon cinnamon

METHOD

■ Cook the peeled apples to a purée (see Applesauce on page 135), transfer to a large bowl, and allow to cool slightly.

■ Preheat the oven to 450°F (232°C), and grease the loaf pan. Combine the flour, spices, and salt in a mixing bowl. Dissolve the yeast in the warm water, and then add it and the melted butter to the apple purée.

■ Add one half of the flour mixture to the purée mixture, and stir well. Continue adding the flour, a little at a time, until you can turn the dough out onto a smooth surface. Knead the bread for about 5 minutes, adding flour as necessary, until the dough is smooth. Gently press the dough out into a 1"-thick (2.5 cm) rectangle, roll the rectangle into a loaf shape, and press the seams closed.

■ Place the shaped loaf into the loaf pan, seam side down, and allow it to rise until doubled in volume. Bake for about 35 minutes. The finished loaf will be golden on top and should produce a hollow sound when you thump it on the bottom. Turn out onto a cooling rack.

■ To make the butter, combine the ingredients in a mixer fitted with a paddle blade, and blend on low speed. If the completed butter is well covered and stored in the refrigerator, it will keep for several weeks.

Note: To toast the nuts for the butter, first preheat the oven to 325°F (163°C). Spread the nuts in one even layer on a sheet pan, and place the pan in the middle of the oven for about 15 minutes or until the nuts are golden brown. The toasting time will vary; if the nuts aren't done in 15 minutes, check every 5 minutes until they are. Allow the nuts to cool before grinding them in a blender.

APPLE WALNUT MUFFINS *with* DATE-NUT SPREAD

These delicious muffins are very easy to make, and, when they're served for breakfast with the chopped date-and-marscapone filling, make an entire meal in themselves. Marscapone, in case you've never tasted it before, is an Italian cream cheese.

Yields
12 SERVINGS

Spice grinder (optional)

Mixer with paddle blade

Nonstick muffin pan, oiled muffin pan,
or pan with cupcake liners

SPREAD INGREDIENTS

1/2 cup (118 ml) fresh apple cider

1 cup finely chopped dates

5 whole allspice berries

5 whole coriander seeds

8 ounces (227 g) softened marscapone
(Italian cream cheese)

3 whole, pitted dates

Note: If you don't own a spice grinder, just use 1/4 teaspoon each of ground allspice and coriander instead of whole berries and seeds.

MUFFIN INGREDIENTS

1 cup (120 g) ground English walnuts

1/2 cup (60 g) ground black walnuts

1-1/2 (180 g) cups all-purpose flour

6 tablespoons baking powder

1/4 teaspoon salt

3/4 cup (150 g) granulated sugar

3 eggs

6 tablespoons unsalted butter, melted

1-1/2 cups (355 ml) warm milk

1-1/2 cups (170 g) diced apples

■ Pour the cider into a saucepan. Add the chopped dates, and simmer over medium heat for 5 minutes. Set aside to cool.

■ Combine the allspice berries and coriander seeds, and grind them to a powder in a spice grinder. Whip the marscapone in the mixer until fluffy. Add the spices, and blend. To complete the spread, add the cooled date mixture, and beat until smooth. Place in a small dish, and garnish with the whole, pitted dates.

■ Preheat the oven to 350°F (177°C). Combine the ground walnuts, flour, baking powder, salt, and sugar in a mixing bowl. Mix together the eggs, melted butter, and warm milk in another bowl, and beat lightly with a fork or wire whisk. Add the egg mixture and the diced apples to the dry ingredients, and use a wooden spoon or rubber spatula to mix. Let stand 10 minutes.

■ Fill the cups of a nonstick muffin pan with the batter. Bake 10 minutes or until a toothpick inserted into the center of a muffin comes out clean. Serve warm or cold.

RAISED WAFFLES *with* CIDER CINNAMON SYRUP

These yeasted waffles, which offer a wonderful combination of light and crispy textures, are also excellent as a dessert served with Cider Lemon Sorbet (see pages 112–113). The basic batter—without the eggs and baking soda—can be refrigerated for several days.

Yields

6 WAFFLES AND 1 CUP (237 ML) SYRUP

BASIC RECIPE INCLUDED

Apple Cider Reduction
with cinnamon and cloves
(PAGE 132)

HAVE ON HAND

Cheesecloth or clean kitchen towel

Waffle iron

INGREDIENTS

1/2 cup (118 ml) warm water

1 tablespoon yeast

2 cups (473 ml) warm milk

1/2 cup (115 g) butter, melted

2 cups (250 g) all-purpose flour

1/2 teaspoon salt

1 teaspoon granulated sugar

2 eggs

1/4 teaspoon baking soda

Apple Cider Reduction

Plain yogurt

Cinnamon

METHOD

■ The evening before your planned waffle breakfast, place the warm water in a large mixing bowl, and dissolve the yeast in it. Add the warm milk and melted butter.

■ In a separate bowl, combine the flour, salt, and sugar. Add these dry ingredients to the wet ingredients, and beat until smooth. Cover the bowl, and allow the batter to stand overnight at room temperature.

■ The next morning, preheat the waffle iron. Just prior to cooking the waffles, beat the eggs well, fold them into the batter, and then beat in the baking soda. Pour the very thin batter into the heated waffle iron, and cook until golden brown.

■ Serve with the apple cider reduction, plain yogurt, and a dusting of cinnamon.

Note: When you make the Apple Cider Reduction, which will serve as the syrup, you may want to add a dash of cayenne.

CRISPY POTATO PANCAKES
with APPLESAUCE *and* GOAT CHEESE

If you yearn for a reputation as a great cook, treat your friends to a late breakfast serving of these wonderful and very simple pancakes.

Yields
6 SERVINGS

BASIC RECIPE INCLUDED

Applesauce
(PAGE 135)

HAVE ON HAND

Ovenproof dish

INGREDIENTS

4 large potatoes, peeled and grated (see "Note")

10 tablespoons (145 g) clarified butter, melted

2 tablespoons cider vinegar

2 shallots, peeled and finely diced

1/2 cup (118 ml) fresh apple cider

1/2 cup (118 ml) heavy cream

6 ounces (170 g) goat cheese, cut into 12 thin slices

1-1/2 cups (355 ml) Applesauce

1 tablespoon grainy mustard

Several tablespoons chopped, fresh chives

METHOD

■ Preheat a heavy skillet over medium heat. In a mixing bowl, toss the potatoes with one-half the melted butter. Add the remaining melted butter to the skillet. Divide the grated potatoes into 18 equal portions, making a small mound with each one. Drop the mounds into the heated butter, and fry for about 5 minutes on each side, or until crispy. Keep in mind that slow cooking is better than fast; hot, rapid cooking may burn the potato cakes rather than crisp them. Remove from the pan, drain, and reserve.

■ To make the sauce, place the cider vinegar and shallots in a saucepan over medium heat. Reduce the vinegar by two-thirds; the finished reduction should be as thick as syrup. Add the apple cider, and reduce by half. Add the heavy cream, turn the heat down, and simmer for 15 minutes.

■ Preheat the oven to 350°F (177°C). In an ovenproof dish, make 6 three-cake-high stacks as follows: Start each stack with a potato cake, top it with a slice of goat cheese, and place a dollop of applesauce on the cheese, continuing to layer the cakes, cheese slices, and applesauce until all the stacks are completed. Then place the dish in the oven for about 8 minutes to reheat.

■ Just before serving, stir the mustard and 3 tablespoons of the chives into the sauce, and spoon a little onto each serving plate. Place a stack of cakes on top, and finish each stack with another dollop of applesauce. Garnish with the remaining chives.

Note: Do not rinse the peeled potatoes—their starch will hold the cakes together.

Apple, Cheddar, and Spinach Omelet with Tiny Apple Pancakes, Apple Yogurt, and Cider Syrup

There's nothing more satisfying than a weekend brunch after all the work is done and all the kids have gone out to play. Here's a delicious recipe combination for such occasions. Enjoy it with a sparkling cider. And don't be shocked. I use a pancake mix to make my weekend life easier.

Yields
2 SERVINGS

BASIC RECIPES INCLUDED

Applesauce
(PAGE 135)

Apple Cider Reduction
(PAGE 132)

HAVE ON HAND

Omelet pan

FILLING INGREDIENTS

*1 tart eating apple, peeled,
cored, and grated*

2 tablespoons lemon juice

1-1/2 tablespoons butter

1/2 cup (90 g) steamed, drained spinach

1/8 teaspoon nutmeg

1/8 teaspoon cayenne pepper

1/2 teaspoon salt

1/4 cup (28 g) grated white cheddar cheese

OMELET INGREDIENTS

6 eggs

1 teaspoon salt

1/2 teaspoon black pepper

3 tablespoons heavy cream

1/4 cup (28 g) grated white cheddar cheese

4 tablespoons butter

PANCAKE AND CIDER SYRUP INGREDIENTS

1 cup (120 g) whole-wheat pancake mix

1 cup (237 ml) milk

1 egg, lightly beaten

6 tablespoons Applesauce

1/4 teaspoon cinnamon

1/4 teaspoon nutmeg

1/2 cup (118 ml) plain yogurt

1/2 cup (118 ml) Apple Cider Reduction

■ To begin preparing the filling, toss the grated apple with the lemon juice. Melt the butter in a skillet over medium heat. When the foam of the butter subsides, toss in the apples, and sauté until soft. Add the spinach, and season with nutmeg, cayenne, and salt. Cook just long enough to heat through. Remove from the heat, mix in the grated cheese, and set aside.

■ To make 2 omelets, complete the following process twice. Break 3 of the eggs into a bowl, and add one-half the salt, pepper, cream, and cheese. Beat the egg mixture lightly with a fork.

■ In an omelet pan over medium heat, melt 2 tablespoons of the butter. When the foam subsides, pour the egg mixture in all at once. As the omelet cooks for about 2 minutes, use a rubber spatula to pull its edges in toward the center. Then spread one-quarter of the filling onto one-half of the omelet, and fold the other half of the omelet over to cover the filling. Cook until the bottom of the omelet is golden brown, then flip the omelet over, and brown the other side as well.

■ Combine the pancake mix, milk, egg, and 3 tablespoons of applesauce. Flavor with half of the cinnamon and nutmeg, reserving the remainder for the yogurt. Make small pancakes, each about 3" (7.6 cm) in diameter, and keep warm.

■ Mix the remaining applesauce and spices with the yogurt, and set aside, along with the apple cider reduction, until you're ready to serve the meal.

■ Place the finished omelets onto warm dishes, and surround each one with pancakes. Top the pancakes with the yogurt, and serve the apple cider reduction separately as a syrup.

Notes: The best way to prepare this meal is with someone else, so that one person can cook the eggs while the other person cooks the pancakes.

The two tricks to making perfect omelets are to add a little heavy cream to the eggs, and to avoid cooking over heat that is too high. Excessively high temperatures will leave you with eggs that are hard and crumbly instead of creamy and melting.

APPLE *and* SMOKED DUCK STRUDEL *with* CIDER *and* TARRAGON SAUCE

There's significant work involved in making this strudel (be sure to read the "Notes" on page 36 before starting), but the basic duckling recipe can be used in many other dishes. Of course, presmoked duck breast makes an adequate substitute for meat that you smoke yourself, but it can be difficult to find and quite expensive. What's more, it's not as much fun to prepare!

Yields
6 SERVINGS

BASIC RECIPES INCLUDED

Cider Verjus
(OPTIONAL; PAGE 133)

Apple Cider Reduction
(PAGE 132)

Apple and Leek Stock
(OPTIONAL; PAGE 134)

10" x 12" (25.5 x 30.5 cm) ovenproof dish, with lid or foil

Charcoal smoker and 1 cup charcoal

Hickory or apple wood, for added flavor and smoke

Sharp boning knife

STRUDEL INGREDIENTS

1 whole 5-pound (2.3 kg) duckling

2 tablespoons salt

6-1/2 teaspoons chopped, fresh thyme

Salt and black pepper to taste

4 cups (946 ml) light cooking oil

1 clove garlic, peeled

1/4 head Napa cabbage

2 tablespoons light cooking oil

1 small onion, thinly sliced

1/2 teaspoon salt

1/2 teaspoon black pepper

1 tart eating apple, peeled, cored, and cut into 1/8" (3 mm) cubes

1 tablespoon fresh tarragon leaves

1 cup (120 g) toasted pecan pieces

3 tablespoons Apple Cider Reduction (thick)

3 tablespoons cider vinegar or Cider Verjus

Salt and black pepper to taste

6 sheets phyllo dough

4 tablespoons butter, melted

SAUCE AND GARNISH INGREDIENTS

1/2 cup (118 ml) cider vinegar or Cider Verjus

1 cup (237 ml) fresh apple cider

2 cups (473 ml) Apple and Leek Stock, chicken stock, or duck stock

1 tablespoon chopped, fresh tarragon

Salt and black pepper to taste

2 tablespoons butter, softened

1/4 cup (30 g) toasted pecan pieces

■ Using a sharp knife, remove the duckling's leg-and-thigh sections, keeping each leg and thigh paired in a single piece. Rub the 2 pieces with 2 tablespoons of salt and 2 tablespoons of the chopped thyme, place in the ovenproof dish, cover the dish, and refrigerate overnight. Reserve the remainder of the duck.

■ On the second day, preheat the oven to 450°F (232°C). Season the whole duck section (minus the leg-and-thigh pieces) with salt, pepper, and the remaining thyme, or substitute another favorite herb—rosemary or lavender, for example—if you like. Place this portion of the duck in a roasting pan, and roast it, breast side up, for 35 minutes; the breast should still be pink. Remove from the oven, and allow to cool.

■ Reduce the oven temperature to 300°F (149°C). Cover the leg-and-thigh pieces with about 4 cups of light cooking oil, and add the garlic clove. Cover the baking dish, and cook the pieces for about 1-1/2 hours or until the meat begins to shrink away from the bones and is tender when pierced with a fork. Remove from the oven, and place on a rack to cool and drain.

■ For this recipe, you'll need to use a sharp boning knife to remove each breast in one piece. Start at the back end of the breast (the end farthest from the wishbone), and make a shallow incision next to and along one side of the breast bone, all the way to the neck. Continue to follow the breast bone down, until the breast is free from the bone. Repeat the process to remove the other breast piece.

■ The next step is smoking the breasts. Soak the wood in water for 1 hour; drain it 1/2 hour before using. Build a small charcoal fire, using 1 cup of charcoal. Place the soaked and drained wood on the charcoal just prior to placing the duck breast in the smoker. Smoke the breast pieces for 1 hour, and allow them to cool.

■ The hard work's finished! Now you can start the strudel. Cut the cabbage into a *chiffonade* (ribbon-like pieces). Place 2 tablespoons of oil, the cabbage, and the onion slices in a heavy skillet over medium heat. Cook the vegetables only long enough for them to wilt and give up some of their moisture—this is called sweating. Do not allow them to brown. Season with 1/2 teaspoon each of salt and pepper, and place into a mixing bowl.

■ Toss the apple cubes in with the cabbage-and-onion mixture. Add the tarragon and toasted pecan pieces.

■ Pull the duckling meat from the leg-and-thigh pieces, chop it finely, and add it to the mixture. Cut one of the smoked breasts into thin strips, and add it as well. (The other breast will be sliced and used as a garnish.) Finally, add the apple cider reduction, the vinegar or verjus, and salt and pepper to taste.

■ Preheat the oven to 425°F (218°C). Brush the tops of the phyllo sheets liberally with melted butter, one sheet at a time. Fold a sheet of pastry in half, and brush with butter again. (The secret to flaky phyllo is to brush all exposed areas generously with butter.)

■ Place one-sixth of the mixture at one end of the dough, leaving about 1" (2.5 cm) of uncovered dough at each edge. Fold these edges toward the middle, over the duck mixture, and then roll the strudel to make a closed package. Brush with butter. Repeat to make the other 5 strudels. Place the strudels on a buttered baking sheet, and bake for 20 minutes, until the dough is golden and crispy.

■ While the strudels are baking, prepare the sauce. First, in a saucepan placed over high heat, reduce the cider vinegar or verjus by half (to 1/4 cup or 59 ml). Add the fresh apple cider, and reduce again by half. Add the stock and tarragon, and reduce to 1 cup. Season with salt and pepper. Just before serving, whip in the softened butter.

■ To serve this dish, cut the thinnest of slices off each end of each strudel. Then cut each strudel in half diagonally, and stand the halves on their flat ends. Place a slice or two of the remaining duck breast on each plate, sprinkle with a few pecans, and ladle a little of the sauce over the top. Serve hot.

Notes: Two different methods are used to prepare the duck in this recipe. Some of the meat is roasted, and some is prepared as a *confit,* traditionally defined as a meat that has been cooked and preserved in its own fat. The confit method is still used extensively, especially in regions of France where *foie gras* (the fattened livers of moulard ducks) is popular.

The oil-cured duck meat can be used in hundreds of different ways, and if it's left in the oil, allowed to cool, and placed in the refrigerator, it will keep for months. To prepare it for use, just remove the meat from the fat, allow it to warm slightly so that the excess oil will drain away, and then grill or roast it until crisp, serving with sauce if desired.

MUSIC AND REFRESHMENTS

GEORGE COCHRAN LAMBDIN
NEW YORK STATE HISTORICAL ASSOCIATION, COOPERSTOWN, NY

Have you ever wondered how to tell whether an apple is ripe or not? You can bite into it, of course, and let your tongue do the testing, but what tastes good to you may not taste good to some-

If the apple has been fully pollinated, you'll find two seeds in each chamber. If there are fewer than a total of ten seeds, the apple hasn't been fully pollinated and may be lopsided.

one else. I like a crisp, tart apple for eating; other people enjoy riper apples, in which the conversion of starch to sugar is more complete. Your definition of ripeness will also depend on how you intend to use the apple. A delicious, tart eating apple may not be ripe enough for cider making, in which very well-ripened, mellow apples are essential.

As apples ripen—a process that may take from several days to several weeks—some of the changes they go through are visible and others are not. Their skins lose chlorophyll, and the orange and red pigments in them increase. Their flesh becomes softer, their starch content and acidity decrease, and their sweetness, flavor, aroma, and juiciness increase.

Let's take a look at one of the visual changes that ripening apples undergo. Slice an apple in half along its equator. You'll see two distinctly different parts: the fleshy portion that we think of as food; and the "true" apple—the core where the seeds are contained. The core consists of five seed chambers (an area known as the *carpel*), which are arranged in a starlike pattern.

At the periphery of the carpel, you'll notice some small points or dots. These are called *vascular bundles* and are the forms left by the petals and sepals of the apple blossom. The bundles are connected by a ring (not always visible), which marks the outer margin of the core. As the apple ripens, the core or "true" apple feeds upon the same fleshy portion of the apple that we enjoy, and the ring, with its points or dots, gradually migrates out towards the apple's skin. The farther out the ring, the more complete the conversion of starch to sugar within the apple—and the riper the apple is.

SEA SCALLOPS *with* CORIANDER *and* CIDER SAUCE

Whether you serve it as the elegant first course of a formal dinner or as a luncheon dish, this recipe takes very little time to prepare.

Yields
6 SERVINGS

INGREDIENTS

30 large sea scallops
(see "Note")

4 tablespoons coriander

1 teaspoon salt

1/2 teaspoon black pepper

1/4 teaspoon nutmeg

1 large leek, white part only

3 tablespoons light cooking oil

1/2 cup (118 ml) fresh apple cider

1-1/2 cups (355 ml) fish or shrimp stock

1/4 cup (59 ml) dry white Riesling

1"-long (2.5 cm) piece of ginger,
peeled and finely chopped

1 tablespoon whole coriander seeds

3 sprigs fresh thyme leaves

Zest of 1 lemon

2 tablespoons butter

METHOD

■ Combine the coriander, salt, pepper, and nutmeg. Set aside 1 teaspoon of this mixture to garnish the finished dish. Pat the scallops dry, dip both sides of each one into the mixture, and set the coated scallops aside while you make the sauce and garnish.

■ Cut the leek into 1"-long (2.5 cm) julienne strips. Heat 1 tablespoon of the cooking oil in a sauté pan over medium heat; then "sweat" the leek strips until they're soft. Don't allow them to take on any color. Set aside and keep warm.

■ To make the sauce, first combine the cider, stock, and wine. Then add the ginger, coriander seeds, and thyme. Bring the mixture to a slow boil, and reduce to 1-1/2 cups (355 ml). Strain and return to the pan. Add the lemon zest, keeping the sauce at the simmering point.

■ Heat the remaining 2 tablespoons of oil in a heavy skillet over medium-high heat. Cook the scallops for 3 minutes on each side.

■ Just before serving, return the sauce to a boil, and whip in the butter with a wire whisk. Spoon some sauce into each of 6 serving plates. Make 5 little beds of leeks in the sauce on each plate, and top each one with a scallop. Dust the dish with the reserved coriander mixture, and serve at once.

Note: When you sauté the scallops, either use a pan large enough to leave space between them, or cook them in batches. If you add too many to the pan at one time, the cooking temperature will drop, and the scallops will steam instead of sauté. Their outer surfaces should be crispy.

ROASTED SALMON *with* RED-ONION-*and*-APPLE PURÉE CRUST *and* GINGER BUTTER SAUCE

This recipe was developed by Joe Trull, who worked in my kitchen for many years; it serves as testimony to Joe's ear for jazz. The subtle way in which the flavors harmonize is nothing less than jazzy.

Yields
6 SERVINGS

Red-Onion-and-Apple Purée
(PAGE 133)

HAVE ON HAND

Two 12"-long (30.5 cm) pieces of smooth cedar board

7" (17.8 cm) sauté pan

SAUCE INGREDIENTS

3 shallots, peeled and finely diced

1 tablespoon chopped, fresh or pickled ginger

1/4 cup (59 ml) white wine vinegar

1/2 cup (118 ml) white wine

2 tablespoons heavy cream

1 cup (230 g) butter, cut into 1" (2.5 cm) cubes

SALMON INGREDIENTS

6 six-ounce (170 g) salmon filets

2 tablespoons light cooking oil

Salt and black pepper to taste

1 cup (237 ml) Red-Onion-and-Apple Purée

SPINACH AND GARNISH INGREDIENTS

2 cups (360 g) cooked spinach

2 tablespoons butter

1 teaspoon salt

1/2 teaspoon black pepper

1/2 teaspoon grated nutmeg

1/2 lemon

4 diced shallots

■ The ginger butter sauce can be made about 1 hour before serving the meal or, if you work quickly, as the filets are baking. To make the sauce, combine the shallots, ginger, vinegar, and wine in a saucepan. Bring the mixture to a boil over medium heat, and reduce the liquid by two-thirds or until it's the consistency of syrup. If you're making the sauce ahead of time, stop here until your filets are almost ready to serve, removing the sauce from the heat and keeping it warm on top of the stove or in a double boiler. When the filets are almost ready, add the cream to the sauce, return to a boil, and add a few pieces of the butter, whisking them in quickly until they dissolve. Continue whisking in the butter, a few pieces at a time, until it has all been incorporated.

■ To prepare the salmon filets, preheat the oven to 400°F (205°C), and oil the cedar boards with cooking oil. Season each filet with salt and pepper, and place 3 on each board. Spread 1/2 cup (118 ml) of the purée evenly over each set of filets. Place the boards in the oven, and roast for 25 minutes; the boards will blacken but can be washed and reused many times.

■ Make the sautéed spinach several minutes before the salmon is done. Preheat a 7" (17.8 cm) sauté pan over medium heat. Add the butter, and let it melt until it begins to sizzle. Add the cooked spinach, and season with salt, pepper, and nutmeg. Toss to heat through. Just before serving, squeeze the lemon over the spinach, and toss to mix.

■ When the filets are done, transfer them to individual serving dishes, sauce them, and serve with the sautéed spinach. Garnish with diced shallots.

APPLE-STUFFED MOREL BEIGNETS

This decidedly exotic recipe is well worth the effort it requires. Morels are gathered when apple trees are in blossom, and these delectable mushrooms can often be found in old orchards. You needn't search them out yourself, of course; they're available through specialty-food suppliers.

Yields
6 SERVINGS

BASIC RECIPES INCLUDED

Apple Cider Reduction
(PAGE 132)

Applesauce
(PAGE 135)

■ Mix together all the batter ingredients except the egg whites, and whisk until smooth. Cover and refrigerate for at least 3 or 4 but no more than 12 hours.

Pastry bag with a plain, straight tube small enough to fit into the hollow morel stems, about 1/4" (6 mm) in diameter

■ To begin the stuffing, combine the cider and vinegar, and follow the instructions for making an apple cider reduction (see page 132) to create 1 tablespoon of thick glaze. Do be careful not to burn this reduction.

Electric deep fryer or 1-1/2-quart (1.4 l) saucepan, frying thermometer, and at least 1 quart (.9 l) of vegetable frying oil

■ With a fork, mash the rice with the applesauce to form a smooth purée. Add the marjoram and reduced cider glaze, and season with salt and pepper.

BATTER INGREDIENTS

■ Fill the pastry bag with the stuffing, and pipe each morel full. Be careful as you do this; too much pressure on the pastry bag will split the morels open. Set the stuffed morels aside.

1-1/4 cups (156 g) all-purpose flour

1 cup (118 ml) fresh apple cider

■ Next comes the ragoût. In a heavy skillet, heat the butter over medium heat until the foam has subsided. Add the morels and the apples, and season with marjoram, chopped chives, nutmeg, salt, and pepper. Sauté for 15 minutes, until the apples and mushrooms are well browned, turning 3 times to prevent sticking.

1/2 teaspoon lemon zest

1/4 teaspoon salt

1/8 teaspoon black pepper

2 egg whites

■ Add the cider vinegar, and let it evaporate completely. Then add the apple cider, and reduce by half. Remove the ragoût from the heat, and keep warm.

STUFFED MOREL INGREDIENTS

■ Preheat the deep fryer to 375°F (190°C). If you're using a saucepan instead, fill it two-thirds full with oil, and use a frying thermometer to adjust the temperature. Cover a draining rack with absorbent paper.

3/4 cup (177 ml) fresh apple cider

2 tablespoons cider vinegar

1/4 cup (50 g) cooked rice

■ Just before using the batter, thin it if necessary by adding a little water. Then whip the egg whites to the soft-peak stage and fold them in. The finished batter should be the consistency of heavy cream.

3/4 cup (177 ml) Applesauce

1 tablespoon chopped, fresh marjoram leaves

1 teaspoon salt

■ Carefully dip the stuffed morels into the batter, and deep-fry them, 5 at a time, for about 2 minutes or until golden. Using a slotted spoon, remove, drain on the covered rack, and keep warm. Continue until all the morels have been cooked.

1/2 teaspoon white pepper

30 perfect morels, each 3" (7.6 cm) long (see "Note")

■ To serve, divide the ragoût equally among 6 dishes. Arrange 5 morels around the ragoût on each dish, and garnish with whole chives. Top with a bit more ragoût.

RAGOÛT AND GARNISH INGREDIENTS

Note: To clean the morels, first use a kitchen towel or vegetable brush to remove as much dirt as possible. Then rinse under cold running water, drain well, and pat dry.

4 tablespoons butter

2 cups (140 g) whole morels

2 large dessert apples, peeled, cored, and sliced

1/2 teaspoon chopped, fresh marjoram leaves

1 tablespoon chopped, fresh chives

1/2 teaspoon nutmeg

1 teaspoon salt

1/2 teaspoon black pepper

1 tablespoon cider vinegar

1/4 cup (59 ml) fresh apple cider

30 whole chives

PISTACHIO-CRUSTED BREAST *of* FREE-RANGE CHICKEN
STUFFED *with* APPLE-LEEK PURÉE

So what's the big deal about free-range chicken? Basically, it tastes better. There are health advantages to using chickens raised in a natural manner, of course, but for me, the bottom line is always "flavor first." I do not, however, go as far as a French wine-maker friend of mine, who selects only eleven-week-old chickens raised in Bresse, France. He claims that by flexing the breast bones of these chickens, he can distinguish them from all others.

The simple apple-and-leek stuffing, which can be prepared days in advance, is a preparation that I use over and over in my cooking. The combination of apples, leeks, and thyme in it provides an incomparable mixture of flavors and textures.

Yields
6 SERVINGS

Apple and Leek Stock
(OPTIONAL; PAGE 134)

HAVE ON HAND

Meat mallet or heavy sauté pan with
slightly rounded bottom

ROASTED CORN INGREDIENTS

4 ears corn

4 teaspoons butter, melted

1/8 teaspoon salt

1 tablespoon butter or corn oil
(for reheating)

STUFFING INGREDIENTS

2 leeks (white part only)

4 cooking apples, peeled, cored,
and cut into 2" (5.1 cm) cubes

2 tablespoons fresh thyme leaves

2 tablespoons butter

1 teaspoon salt

CHICKEN AND GARNISH
INGREDIENTS

3 free-range chicken breasts,
bones and skin removed

3 cups (710 ml) Apple and Leek Stock
or chicken stock

3 tablespoons butter, melted

2 tablespoons chopped, fresh thyme

1-1/2 cups (180 g) chopped pistachio nuts

Salt and black pepper to taste

3 sprigs fresh marjoram

■ Preheat the oven to 325°F (163°C). Shuck and wash the fresh corn. Brush each ear with 1 teaspoon melted butter, and season with salt. Place the ears on a baking sheet, and roast for 15 minutes. Turn the corn over, and roast an additional 15 to 20 minutes, until light gold in color. Remove and cool. Use a sharp thin-bladed knife to remove the kernels.

■ To begin making the stuffing, wash the leeks to remove all traces of dirt, and slice into thin circles. Then combine all the stuffing ingredients in a heavy saucepan. Cover the pan tightly with a lid or aluminum foil, and place over low heat. Check after 10 minutes. The ingredients should be *sweating* (giving up their moisture). Continue to cook for an additional 35 minutes (leave the lid on), until the leeks are soft enough to be mashed with a fork. Check every 5 minutes to make sure that the leeks aren't sticking to the bottom of the pan. Remove from the heat, allow to cool, and then purée in a blender or food processor, and reserve.

■ Divide each chicken breast in half, and spread the halves out on a sheet of plastic food wrap. Cover with another piece of wrap, and use a meat mallet or the slightly rounded bottom of a heavy sauté pan to flatten them to 1/2" (1.3 cm) in thickness.

■ Remove the upper piece of food wrap, and, on the side of each breast from which you removed the bone, place 3 heaping tablespoons of apple-leek purée along one edge. Roll the chicken around the stuffing to form a log. Wrap each log in a new piece of food wrap, twisting the ends to hold them together. Prick the wrap a few times with the point of a knife.

■ Bring the stock to a simmer in an uncovered saucepan, and then drop the logs in and allow them to simmer for 20 minutes. When the chicken feels firm to the touch, remove and drain, leaving the wrap on. Turn the stock on high, and boil until reduced to about 3/4 cup (177 ml); this reduction will form the sauce.

■ Preheat the oven to 350°F (177°C). Next, combine the thyme and pistachio nuts. Unwrap the breasts, brush with melted butter, season with salt and pepper, and roll in the nut mixture to coat. Place on a buttered baking sheet, and bake for about 20 minutes or until the nuts are golden. Remove and keep warm.

■ To reheat the corn, toss it in a small pan with 1 tablespoon of butter or corn oil until warm. Arrange the kernels in a bed on the serving platter. Slice the logs, arrange on the bed of corn, and pour the reduced stock on top. Arrange any leftover nut mixture around the plate, and garnish with fresh marjoram. Serve immediately.

CIDER BARBECUED SHRIMP
with WHITE BEANS and APPLES

The barbecue sauce recipe included here is an all-round winner and can be adjusted to suit the level of "fire" that you like. If it's refrigerated, the sauce will keep for 2 to 3 months.

Yields
6 MAIN-COURSE SERVINGS OR 12 APPETIZER SERVINGS

BASIC RECIPES INCLUDED

Cider Verjus
(OPTIONAL; PAGE 133)

Apple and Leek Stock
(OPTIONAL; PAGE 134)

Charcoal grill

CIDER BARBECUE
INGREDIENTS

*1 cup (237 ml) cider vinegar
or Cider Verjus*

2 cups (473 ml) fresh apple cider

*2 cups (473 ml) Apple and Leek Stock
or chicken stock*

1/2 cup (118 ml) soy sauce

1/4 cup (59 ml) tomato paste

1 tablespoon peeled, sliced, fresh ginger

2 teaspoons cayenne pepper, more or less

3 whole coriander seeds

*4 sprigs fresh thyme,
leaves picked from stem*

1 bay leaf

SHRIMP WITH WHITE BEANS
INGREDIENTS

36 large shrimp, peeled and deveined

2 cups (364 g) dried white navy beans

*2 cups (473 ml) Apple and Leek Stock
or chicken stock*

1 cup (237 ml) fresh apple cider

1-1/2 teaspoons salt

1 teaspoon black pepper

3 sprigs fresh thyme

2 sprigs fresh marjoram

*4 tablespoons finely diced onion
(optional)*

*4 tablespoons finely diced celery
(optional)*

*4 tablespoons finely diced carrot
(optional)*

2 cups (360 g) spinach, cooked

■ Soak the beans overnight in cold water.

■ Reduce the cider vinegar or verjus to 1/4 cup (59 ml) in a saucepan over high heat. Add the remaining cider barbecue ingredients, bring to a boil, and simmer until reduced by two-thirds. About 2 cups (473 ml) of thick, rich sauce should remain. Strain and reserve.

■ Drain and rinse the beans once, and place in a stockpot with the stock, cider, and enough cold water to cover. Add the salt, pepper, thyme, marjoram, and optional vegetables.

■ Place the stockpot over medium heat, and bring to a simmer. Skim and discard the foam that rises to the top. Simmer the beans for about 2 hours or until tender, adding water as necessary to keep them covered with liquid. Remove the beans from the stove, and allow them to absorb any liquid that remains.

■ The best way to barbecue the shrimp is to poach them first. Bring a pot of water to a boil, and drop the shrimp in all at once. Watch the shrimp closely; as soon as they turn pink, drain them and run them under cold water. Allow the cool shrimp to drain for several minutes.

■ Place the drained shrimp in a shallow dish, brush them with cider barbecue sauce, and allow them to marinate, unrefrigerated, for 30 minutes. Then grill the shrimp over a charcoal grill, about 2 minutes per side, brushing with additional sauce.

■ Reheat the beans with a little of the sauce, and warm the cooked spinach. To serve, make a ring of spinach around the plate, spoon a portion of beans into the middle, and place the shrimp on top, serving 3 shrimp as an appetizer portion or 6 as a main course.

Note: You'll need to plan this dish in advance, as the dried beans must be soaked for several hours.

APPLE *and* CHICKEN TIMBALES

Suitable for a first course at a formal dinner party, this elegant dish is an excellent choice because it's easy to make and can be prepared well in advance.

Yields
6 SERVINGS

Apple Cider Reduction
(PAGE 132)

Apple and Leek Stock
(OPTIONAL: PAGE 134)

HAVE ON HAND

*6 four-ounce (118 ml) timbale molds
(see "Notes")*

*Shallow baking dish large enough
to hold the molds*

TIMBALE INGREDIENTS

*2 whole chicken breasts,
bones and skin removed*

*2 tart cooking apples, peeled,
cored, and chopped*

*1 cup (237 ml) Apple and Leek Stock
or chicken stock*

*2 tablespoons Apple Cider Reduction
(see "Notes")*

1/4 teaspoon nutmeg

1/4 teaspoon ginger

1/4 teaspoon cloves

2 teaspoons salt

1/2 teaspoon white pepper

1 egg white

SAUCE AND GARNISH INGREDIENTS

2 tablespoons cider vinegar

1/2 cup (118 ml) fresh apple cider

3 tablespoons diced onion

3 sprigs chopped, fresh thyme

*1 cup (237 ml) Apple and Leek Stock or
chicken stock*

1/8 teaspoon nutmeg

1/8 teaspoon ginger

1/8 teaspoon cloves

1 eating apple, peeled, cored, and diced

Fresh thyme leaves

2 tablespoons butter, softened (optional)

■ Preheat the oven to 375°F (190°C). Place the chopped apples in a saucepan, cover tightly, and cook over medium-low heat for 15 minutes or until soft.

■ Remove the tough, fibrous tendon from the inside of each chicken breast, and cut the meat into 1/2" (1.3 cm) cubes. Combine the chicken and cooked apples, and place the mixture in a food processor or blender. Turn the processor on for 15 seconds, adding about 1/2 of the stock and all of the cider reduction. Turn off the processor. Add the spices and seasonings, scrape down the sides of the processor with a rubber spatula, and turn the processor back on for 15 to 20 seconds, continuing to add stock until the mixture is light and creamy. The exact amount of stock required will vary. The finished purée should be as thick as sour cream. Scrape the processor again, making sure that all the chicken is puréed. Add the egg white, and process for another 5 seconds.

■ Grease the timbale molds with vegetable oil or butter. Divide the timbale mixture among the 6 molds, and place the molds in a shallow baking dish. Pour hot water into the dish to reach halfway up the sides of the molds. Bake for 30 minutes, until the mixture is set and firm to the touch, and remove. Leave the cooked timbales in their molds. (They can be refrigerated for up to 3 days.)

■ To make the sauce, first reduce the cider vinegar, apple cider, onion, and thyme to make 1/4 cup (59 ml) of liquid. Add the stock, and simmer until reduced by one-third. As the stock cooks, add the spices. Strain and return to the saucepan, and reduce by one-half. Add the diced apple at the end of the reduction, and keep the sauce warm.

■ Reheat the timbales in their molds by placing the molds in a shallow pan filled with simmering water for 10 minutes, either in the oven or on top of the stove. If you reheat them in the oven, preheat to 350°F (177°C).

■ Unmold the timbales onto a serving dish, ladle a little of the sauce on top, and garnish with fresh thyme leaves. (To make the sauce richer, whip in 2 tablespoons of softened butter just before serving.)

Notes: When you make the apple cider reduction called for in the timbale mixture, follow the instructions provided on page 132, but use 3/4 cup cider and 2 tablespoons cider vinegar instead of the amounts called for in that basic recipe.

Timbale molds, which are small and tapered, are 1-1/2" (3.8 cm) in diameter and 3" (7.6 cm) in height, and can be found at many kitchen-supply shops. If you don't want to purchase them, substitute any 4-ounce (118 ml) molds.

APPLE-STUFFED TROUT *with* WALNUT CRUST

In the spring, I like to substitute wild mountain ramps—pungent, garlic-flavored onions—for the much milder onions in this recipe. The fish may be cooked in batches or in a heavy skillet that is large enough to hold them all.

Yields
6 SERVINGS

6 whole, fresh-water trout, bones removed

2 cooking apples, peeled, cored, and sliced

2 medium onions, thinly sliced

1-1/2 cups (180 g) English walnuts:
1-1/4 cups (150 g) ground into meal
and the remaining 1/4 cup (30 g)
reserved for garnish

1/2 cup (60 g) ground black walnut meal

3 tablespoons chopped,
fresh marjoram leaves

2 large potatoes, peeled and cut
into 3/4" (1.9 cm) cubes

9 tablespoons butter

Salt and black pepper to taste

2 eating apples, peeled, cored, and cut
into 3/4" (1.9 cm) cubes

1/4 cup (31 g) all-purpose flour

Salt and black pepper to taste

3 tablespoons light cooking oil

1 tablespoon chopped,
fresh marjoram leaves

2 lemons

■ To make the stuffing, place the cooking apples and one-third of the sliced onions in a saucepan, and cook them over medium heat until soft; don't let them turn into sauce. Remove from the heat, and mix in 1/2 cup (60 g) of the English walnut meal, 2 tablespoons of the black walnut meal, and 1 tablespoon of the fresh marjoram. Allow to cool.

■ To prepare the potato, onion, and apple garnish, first sauté the potatoes in 3 tablespoons of butter for 10 minutes, using a heavy skillet over medium-low heat. Then add the remaining sliced onions and continue to brown for an additional 15 minutes, turning every 3 to 4 minutes. Season with salt and pepper to taste. Add the cubed eating apples and the 1/4 cup of English walnut pieces, heat through for 3 or 4 minutes, toss in 1 tablespoon of fresh marjoram, and keep warm until ready to serve.

■ Next, combine the remaining walnut meals and the all-purpose flour. Season with salt and pepper. Spread this mixture out on a baking sheet.

■ Divide the apple stuffing evenly between the 6 trout, filling the boned cavity of each fish. Lightly brush the outside of the trout with about 1 tablespoon of the cooking oil, and then roll the trout in the meal-and-flour mixture to coat completely.

■ Melt 4 tablespoons of butter and the remaining 2 tablespoons of cooking oil in a large heavy skillet over medium heat. Sauté the trout for 8 minutes on each side over medium-high heat; the walnuts should turn golden, and the trout flesh should be white. (To check, gently lift up one side of the fish, and peek inside.) Some of the meal will fall off while the fish cooks, but don't worry. Just remove and discard this excess meal before it burns.

■ Move the sautéed fish to a baking pan or platter. Wipe all the loose and blackened material from the skillet. Return the fish to the pan and arrange the potato, onion, and apple garnish around the fish. Place the pan over low heat to keep it warm.

■ Over medium-high heat, preheat a small pan, and cook the remaining 2 tablespoons of butter until it sizzles and begins to turn a nut-brown color. Squeeze the lemons into the butter, toss in the remaining marjoram, and pour over the fish. Serve immediately.

PAUPIETTE *of* VEAL *with* APPLE CHUTNEY

A *paupiette* (or little package) usually consists of a flattened piece of beef, pork, veal, or poultry filled with a stuffing. The key to the recipe provided here is making the *escalope* (thinly sliced and pounded meat). While this dish calls for veal, slices of pork or beef make good substitutes. Less tender cuts, such as the top round of veal or beef, are perfectly acceptable.

Yields
6 SERVINGS AND 5 CUPS (1.2 L) CHUTNEY

BASIC RECIPE INCLUDED

Apple and Leek Stock
(OPTIONAL; PAGE 134)

Meat mallet or heavy sauté pan with
slightly rounded bottom

Butcher's twine or cotton string

9" x 12" (22.0 x 30.5 cm) casserole dish

APPLE CHUTNEY INGREDIENTS

4 cups (454 g) diced, medium-tart apples

1/4 cup (59 ml) cider vinegar

1/4 cup (55 g) light brown sugar

4 tablespoons dark molasses

2 cloves garlic, peeled and finely diced

1 bay leaf

1 hot green chili, stemmed, seeded,
and chopped

3 whole cloves

1 teaspoon green peppercorns

1/2 teaspoon cinnamon

1/4 teaspoon nutmeg

1/2 teaspoon salt

1/4 teaspoon black pepper

PAUPIETTE INGREDIENTS

12 two-ounce (57 g) slices of
top round of veal

1 teaspoon cinnamon

1 teaspoon nutmeg

1/2 teaspoon turmeric

1 teaspoon salt

3 cups (710 ml) Apple Chutney

3 tablespoons light cooking oil

1/2 cup (118 ml) fresh apple cider

1/2 cup (118 ml) Apple and Leek Stock
or chicken stock

3 cups (528 g) cooked Swiss chard

2 cups (358 g) cooked couscous
(see "Note")

METHOD

■ Combine all the chutney ingredients in a saucepan, and cook—covered—for 30 minutes over low heat, stirring occasionally. Uncover and continue to cook until most of the liquid has evaporated and the chutney is thick. If it gets too dry, just add a little water.

■ Using a meat mallet or sauté pan, flatten the slices of veal. Combine the cinnamon, nutmeg, turmeric, and salt, and use this spice mixture to lightly season both sides of each slice of veal. Set aside any remaining mixture.

■ Lay the slices of meat out on the counter. Place 2 tablespoons of chutney on one end of each slice. Fold the sides over the chutney, and roll the slices to make small, closed packages. Secure each paupiette with a length of butcher's twine or thin cotton string.

■ Preheat the oven to 325°F (163°C). In a heavy skillet over medium-high heat, brown the veal in the cooking oil. Then place the paupiettes in a casserole just large enough to hold them in one layer. Add the cider, stock, and any remaining spice mixture, and bring to a simmer on top of the stove. Cover the casserole, and braise it in the oven for 30 minutes. Keep the meat warm until serving time.

■ To serve, warm the remaining chutney and the chard in the oven or on top of the stove. Divide equally among 6 dinner plates. Slice the paupiettes, and divide among the plates, garnishing each plate with couscous. Place the casserole on the stove over high heat, and reduce the liquid to 1/2 cup. Spoon this over the veal, and serve.

Note: Couscous—a grain used in Middle Eastern cookery and now available in most grocery stores—is very easy to cook. Simply boil water and stir in the grain, using the proportions recommended on the package.

RAVIOLI *of* APPLES *and* PANCETTA

Of all my food inventions, I'm inclined to think that this one—the first of my cider inspirations—will outlive me. Note that the sauce is similar to the sauce recipe for Crispy Potato Pancakes (see page 31).

Yields
6 APPETIZER SERVINGS

BASIC RECIPE INCLUDED

Apple Cider Reduction
(PAGE 132)

RAVIOLI INGREDIENTS

2 tablespoons hazelnut oil

*3/4 cup (171 g) finely diced pancetta,
smoked bacon, or prosciutto*

1 leek, white part only, thinly sliced

*2 large eating apples, peeled, cored, and
finely diced*

1 tablespoon chopped, fresh thyme

1 teaspoon black pepper

2 tablespoons Apple Cider Reduction

1 teaspoon Calvados (apple brandy)

*48 goza wrappers
(see "Notes")*

1 egg, lightly beaten

SAUCE AND GARNISH INGREDIENTS

2 tablespoons cider vinegar

1/2 cup (118 ml) fresh apple cider

1-1/2 cups (355 ml) heavy cream

2 tablespoons chopped fresh thyme

1/3 of the ravioli filling

*6 tablespoons (30 g) freshly grated
Parmesan cheese*

METHOD

■ Start by making the ravioli filling. Heat the hazelnut oil in a heavy skillet over medium heat, and sauté the pancetta until brown and crispy. Add the leek and apple, and as they're cooking, add the thyme and pepper. When the leeks are soft, add the apple cider reduction and Calvados. Cook for 2 more minutes, and remove from the heat. Set aside one-third of the mixture for the sauce.

■ To assemble the ravioli, spread out half of the goza wrappers on a clean counter top, and brush them lightly with beaten egg. Place 1/2 teaspoon of filling in the center of each one. Then take a wrapper from the other set of 24, brush it with egg, and press the egg-washed side down onto a filled wrapper. Repeat to assemble the remaining ravioli. Seal by pressing all edges closed with a fork.

■ Before you make the sauce, bring 3 quarts (2.8 l) of lightly salted water to a rolling boil for the ravioli. Also warm the individual serving dishes.

■ Reduce the cider vinegar and cider in a saucepan over medium heat for about 8 to 10 minutes; the reduction should be as thick as syrup. Add the heavy cream and thyme, turn down the heat to a simmer, and reduce slightly. Add the reserved ravioli filling, and keep warm until ready to use.

■ Drop the assembled ravioli into the boiling water, separating them with a fork. Cook for 4 minutes, place in a strainer, and drain well.

■ Place 4 ravioli on each warmed dish, top with sauce and Parmesan cheese, and serve immediately.

Notes: The filled, uncooked ravioli can be prepared in advance, as they'll freeze exceptionally well for up to 2 weeks and can be refrigerated for 2 days. When you store them, separate the layers with pieces of food film or waxed paper. Goza wrappers will stick to each other, so don't let them touch!

You'll find the goza wrappers in the freezers of many Asian food stores. Buy 2 skins for each ravioli. For 6 appetizer servings of 4 ravioli each, you'll need a total of 48 wrappers (about 1 package).

CIDER SMOKED LONDON BROIL
with CIDER PEPPER GLAZE

This recipe combines three intense flavors: smoky beef, sweet cider, and hot pepper. It's a very rich dish—definitely interesting enough to serve on special occasions. For instructions on smoking meat, turn to the recipe for smoked duck on page 35.

Yields
6 SERVINGS

BASIC RECIPE INCLUDED

Cider Verjus
(PAGE 133)

Charcoal smoker and 1 cup charcoal

Hickory or apple wood

INGREDIENTS

1-1/2 pounds (680 g) London broil

*1/2 cup (118 ml) cider vinegar
or Cider Verjus*

1 cup (237 ml) fresh apple cider

3 tablespoons Calvados (apple brandy)

1 tablespoon black pepper

2 tablespoons light cooking oil

2 large potatoes, peeled and thinly sliced

4 tablespoons butter, melted

2 cups (70 g) small button mushrooms

3 tablespoons butter

2 tablespoons chopped, fresh chives

2 tablespoons chopped, fresh marjoram

1/4 teaspoon grated nutmeg

1 teaspoon salt

1/2 teaspoon black pepper

2 tablespoons Madeira

*2 tablespoons cider vinegar
or Cider Verjus*

Several whole chives

■ Start by preparing the cider pepper glaze. Combine the vinegar or verjus and the apple cider in a saucepan. Bring to a boil over high heat, and reduce to 1/2 cup. Add the Calvados, remove from the heat, and stir in the black pepper.

■ Brush both sides of the London broil with the glaze, reserving some for use as a sauce. Allow the meat to sit at room temperature for 1 hour.

■ Before it is smoked, the meat must be seared. Heat the cooking oil in a heavy skillet over medium-high heat. Brown the meat well, searing it for about 5 minutes on each side. Then smoke the seared meat for 30 minutes.

■ While the meat is smoking, preheat the oven to 400°F (205°C), and prepare the potatoes and mushrooms. Toss the potato slices in melted butter. Then make six potato "flowers" by overlapping the slices on a buttered baking sheet. Bake the flowers for 15 to 20 minutes, until golden brown. Set aside.

■ Wash the mushrooms, pat them dry, and cut off their hard stem ends. Melt 3 tablespoons of butter in a heavy skillet over medium heat. Add the mushrooms when the butter sizzles, and cook for 10 minutes or until brown, tossing the mushrooms every 2 or 3 minutes. Add the chives, marjoram, nutmeg, salt, and pepper.

■ When the mushrooms are nicely browned, add the Madeira and cider vinegar or verjus. Continue cooking until the liquid has evaporated. Remove from the heat, and keep warm by placing the pan on the edge of the burner.

■ Place the potato flowers on individual serving dishes. Slice the smoked meat, and divide among the 6 plates. Top with the mushrooms, and drizzle with the reserved glaze. Garnish by topping with whole chives.

Turkey Roulade *with* Sage, Apples, *and* Pine Nuts

Turkey, certainly an underutilized meat, has many benefits for the modern cook. It's low in fat, inexpensive, and most important, when it's included in a good recipe, it tastes great. Apple Ratatouille (see pages 82–83) goes very well with this dish.

Yields
12 SERVINGS

BASIC AND ADDITIONAL
RECIPES INCLUDED

Applesauce
(PAGE 135)

Apple and Leek Stock
(OPTIONAL; PAGE 134)

Apple Ratatouille
(OPTIONAL; PAGES 82–83)

Meat mallet or heavy sauté pan with
slightly rounded bottom

Butcher's twine or cotton string

Meat thermometer

INGREDIENTS

4 pounds (1.8 kg) fresh turkey breast,
bones and skin removed
(see "Note")

3 tablespoons butter

2 cooking apples, peeled, cored,
and cut into 1/2" (1.3 cm) cubes

1/2 cup (75 g) celery, diced

1/2 cup (52 g) leeks (white part only,
thinly sliced)

1 cup (237 ml) Applesauce

1 cup (120 g) toasted pine nuts
(chopped into meal)

1-1/2 teaspoons salt

1 teaspoon black pepper

1 teaspoon cinnamon

4 tablespoons fresh sage leaves

3 egg whites

Salt and pepper to taste

2 quarts (1.9 l) Apple and Leek Stock,
chicken stock, or turkey stock

2 tablespoons butter, softened (optional)

1 tablespoon chopped, fresh sage leaves
(optional)

2 tablespoons light cooking oil

A few fresh sage leaves

■ Place the turkey breast between 2 pieces of plastic food wrap. Using a meat mallet or the bottom of a sauté pan, flatten the breast until it's about 1/2" (1.3 cm) thick. It's best to do this with a number of light but firm smacks. Set the breast aside while you make the stuffing.

■ Melt the butter in a heavy skillet over medium heat. Add the apples, celery, and leeks, and cook for 5 minutes, stirring once every minute, until the ingredients are soft but haven't taken on any color. Place in a mixing bowl.

■ Add the applesauce, pine nuts, salt, pepper, and cinnamon. Cut the sage leaves into fine ribbons, and stir them in as well. Beat the egg whites lightly with a fork, and mix in thoroughly. Chill the mixture for 1 hour.

■ To stuff the roulade, first spread out a 2'-long (61 cm) piece of plastic food wrap. Place the breast, boned side up, at one edge of the wrap. Season the breast with salt and pepper. Spread the stuffing over one-half of the meat, and fold the other half of the breast to cover the stuffing. Roll the breast up, being careful to not to roll the plastic with it. Then wrap the roulade tightly in the plastic sheet, twist the ends of the plastic, and tie each end with cotton twine to secure.

■ Preheat the oven to 400°F (205°C). Bring the stock to a boil, and then turn down to a simmer. Carefully drop the plastic-wrapped roulade into the stock, and poach for 15 minutes. Turn the roulade over, and poach for an additional 15 minutes. To release trapped air, you may need to prick the plastic with a knife point.

■ Using two slotted spoons, lift the roulade out, drain, and place on a cooling rack. (If you've doubled this recipe, allow one of the roulades to cool completely, rewrap it in fresh plastic wrap, cover with aluminum foil, and freeze.)

■ Strain and reserve the stock for some other use, or, if you'd like to make a sauce for this dish, reduce the stock by half. As it is boiling and just before serving, whip in 2 tablespoons of soft butter, and toss in 1 tablespoon of fresh, chopped sage. Remove from the heat and keep warm.

■ Unwrap the cooled roulade, rub it with cooking oil, and roast for 30 minutes, until the outside is browned and the internal temperature is 180°F (82°C). Allow to rest 10 minutes before slicing.

■ To serve, cut into 1/2"-thick (1.3 cm) slices, and garnish with a little stuffing and fresh sage leaves.

Note: A whole turkey breast—bone included—usually weighs about 12 pounds (5.4 kg): 8 pounds (3.6 kg) of meat and 4 pounds (1.8 kg) of bone. Only one side of the boned breast (about 4 pounds or 1.8 kg) of meat is necessary to make this dish. If you buy the whole breast, double the recipe, and freeze one of the roulades for future use. Save the bones for making stock.

Escalope *of* Grouper *with* Apples, Roasted Shallots, *and* Peas

An escalope is a thinly sliced and pounded piece of meat or fish, and can be made from various cuts. In this very quick and very tasty dish, I use a filet of grouper. The key to success, of course, is using only the freshest of fish.

Yields
6 SERVINGS

Meat mallet or heavy sauté pan with
slightly rounded bottom

Small roasting pan

Heavy skillet, 10" to 12"
(25.4 to 30.5 cm) in diameter

INGREDIENTS

1-1/4 pound (567 g) grouper filet

1 teaspoon salt

1 teaspoon black pepper

1 teaspoon coriander

1/4 teaspoon cloves

2 eating apples, peeled, cored, and sliced

Juice of 2 lemons

18 whole shallots, peeled

2 tablespoons light cooking oil

1 cup (226 g) snow peas, strings removed

4 tablespoons butter

1/2 cup (118 ml) fresh apple cider

2 tablespoons Calvados (apple brandy)

■ Preheat the oven to 350°F (177°C). Slice the fish across the width of the filet to create 12 equal 3-ounce (85 g) pieces. Place the slices between two pieces of plastic food wrap. With a meat mallet or the bottom of heavy pan, flatten the filets to 1/2" (1.3 cm) in thickness. Season with salt, pepper, coriander, and cloves, and set aside.

■ Toss the apple slices in the lemon juice, and toss the shallots with 1 tablespoon of the cooking oil. Place the apples and shallots in a small roasting pan, and roast for 20 minutes, turning 3 times, until golden brown. Remove from the oven, and set aside. (This can be done well in advance). Turn the oven down to 225°F (107°C).

■ Blanch the snow peas for 30 seconds in boiling, salted water. Drain, rinse immediately under cold water, and drain well again. Set aside.

■ Preheat the heavy skillet over medium heat, and add the remaining tablespoon of oil and 2 tablespoons of the butter. When the foam of the butter has subsided, add the fish; you may have to cook it in batches, as the escalopes shouldn't be crowded in the skillet. Sauté the fish for 4 minutes on each side. Remove the escalopes, and keep warm on a platter placed in the oven.

■ Discard the butter and oil in the pan, and wipe the pan out with a paper towel. Add the remaining 2 tablespoons of butter, and heat it until it foams. Place the shallots, snow peas, and apples into the pan all at once. Toss for about 30 seconds to heat through, then add the Calvados. Spoon over the grouper, and serve at once.

Sir Isaac Newton's APPLE

You've probably heard that an apple played a prominent role in Isaac Newton's life and thought. Legend has it that as this gentleman reclined under one of the trees in his apple orchard at Woolsthorpe in 1666, the sight of an apple falling nearby prompted his theory of gravity.

Tenaciously as this account has lingered, there's no proof that it's true. Newton may have inadvertently given rise to this story by using the fallen apple as an illustrative metaphor. Nevertheless, in the minds of many, the apple has become forever linked to gravity.

The actual tree from which Newton's apple was thought to have fallen was solemnly preserved for as long as possible, and a descendant of the tree lives on in the Royal Botanical Gardens at Kew, England. Although the name of the apple species has not survived, it was certainly a red apple and probably a *costard*—a variety of large, English cooking apple.

Apple

PAPILLOTE *of* TROUT

Baking in paper containers isn't as popular as it used to be, but it's a technique that every good cook should know. This recipe can also be used with a small pork roast. Just substitute a brown-paper lunch bag for the baking paper, lower the oven temperature to 325°F (163°C) after the first 20 minutes, and increase the cooking time to 1 hour.

Yields
6 SERVINGS

Apple Cider Reduction
(PAGE 132)

HAVE ON HAND

*Six 12" x 12" (30.5 x 30.5 cm) pieces
of baking or silicone paper*

INGREDIENTS

12 six-ounce (170 g) boned trout filets

3 tablespoons light cooking oil

1 carrot, peeled and finely diced

*1 medium red onion, peeled
and finely diced*

*2 cooking apples, peeled, cored,
and finely diced*

1 leek, white part only, cut into julienne

1/2 teaspoon salt

1/2 teaspoon black pepper

*3 tablespoons light cooking oil
for baking paper*

1 tablespoon chopped, fresh thyme

1 tablespoon chopped, fresh parsley

1 teaspoon chopped, fresh tarragon

3 tablespoons Apple Cider Reduction

2 teaspoons cider vinegar

6 tablespoons butter

Apple slices

METHOD

■ Preheat the oven to 375°F (190°C). Heat 3 tablespoons of cooking oil in a heavy skillet over medium heat. Toss in the carrot, onion, apples, and leek, and cook for about 5 minutes or until the vegetables are soft; don't cook them so long that they begin to take on color. Season with salt and pepper. Remove from the heat.

■ To assemble the papillotes, first spread the sheets of baking paper out on a flat surface, and oil them lightly. Place one filet on each piece of paper, positioning it below the center so that you can fold over the upper half of the paper when you're finished. Divide the stuffing among the 6 portions, spreading it evenly on top of each filet. Cover each filet with another filet.

■ Mix together the herbs, apple cider reduction, and cider vinegar, and spread on top of the fish. Dot with butter. Then fold the top half of each sheet of paper downward, make a small series of folds along the meeting edges, and crimp the paper closed. If your packets tend to pop open, use a stapler to close the edges. Place the papillotes on a baking sheet, brush their outer surfaces with cooking oil, and bake for 20 minutes.

■ Remove the papillotes from the oven, slice open the paper, and transfer the fish to serving dishes. Spoon the liquid and remaining stuffing that has collected inside the papillotes over the tops of the fish. Garnish with slices of fresh apple, and serve immediately.

CIDER POT *au* FEU

Poaching—the cooking method used in this recipe—is an oft-neglected technique, but if you follow a few simple rules, it makes a delicious and healthy addition to your cooking repertoire. The rules are provided in the "Note" section of this recipe.

Yields
6 SERVINGS

BASIC RECIPE INCLUDED

Apple and Leek Stock
(OPTIONAL; PAGE 134)

Large saucepan or 6-quart (5.7 l) stockpot

1 stewing chicken

1 teaspoon salt

1/2 teaspoon black pepper

3 sprigs fresh thyme

2 whole coriander seeds

3 sprigs fresh marjoram

2 cups (473 ml) fresh apple cider

*2 cups (473 ml) Apple and Leek Stock
or chicken stock*

1 teaspoon cider vinegar

*2 large potatoes, peeled and cut
into 2" (5.1 cm) cubes*

*2 carrots, peeled and sliced into
1/4"-thick (6 mm) circles*

*1 parsnip, peeled and sliced into
1/4"-thick (6 mm) circles*

*2 leeks, white part only, sliced into
1/4"-thick (6 mm) circles*

1 eating apple, peeled, cored, and sliced

1 tablespoon Calvados (apple brandy)

■ Cut the chicken into 6 pieces, separating the legs from the thighs and splitting the breast in half. (Save the wings and back to make stock.) Remove and discard the skin.

■ Combine the spices, herbs, cider, stock, and vinegar in a pot large enough to hold all the ingredients. Bring to a simmer, add the potatoes, carrots, parsnips, and leeks, and continue to simmer for 30 minutes. Skim any foam that rises to the top.

■ Add the chicken legs and thighs, and simmer for 10 more minutes. Then add the breasts, and simmer for 15 more minutes. Continue to skim any foam throughout the cooking. Add the sliced apple, simmer for a final 5 minutes, and finish the pot au feu by adding the Calvados just before serving.

■ Arrange the vegetables on each plate, place a piece of chicken on top, and spoon some of the broth over the chicken.

Note: Always keep poaching liquid just below the boiling point; never allow it to come to a boil. Watch your timing, too. You want everything to finish cooking at the same time. When planning a poached meal, turn the poaching liquid into a first course by adding fresh vegetables to make a soup.

ROULADE of PORK with APPLE-SAUSAGE STUFFING and APPLES and RED CABBAGE

This is an elegant presentation for special occasions. The roulade can be prepared a day in advance, leaving the final (and easy) roasting for the day of service.

Yields
6 TO 8 SERVINGS (3 CUPS STUFFING)

BASIC RECIPE INCLUDED

Apple and Leek Stock
(OPTIONAL; PAGE 134)

Butcher's twine or cotton string

Meat thermometer

STUFFING INGREDIENTS

1/2 cup (112 g) ground sausage meat

2 stalks celery, finely diced

1/2 bulb fennel, finely diced

1 small tart apple, peeled, cored, and finely diced

1 small red onion, peeled and finely diced

1/4 teaspoon salt

1/4 teaspoon black pepper

1 cup (100 g) bread crumbs

1/2 cup (118 ml) fresh apple cider

ROAST AND POTATO INGREDIENTS

3 pounds (1.4 kg) center-cut pork loin or pork shoulder (see "Notes")

1 tablespoon coriander

1/2 teaspoon ginger

1/2 teaspoon allspice

1/4 teaspoon nutmeg

1/4 teaspoon turmeric

1/4 teaspoon cumin

2 tablespoons light cooking oil

2 or 3 baked potatoes, cut into 1/2"-thick (1.3 cm) slices

1 tablespoon softened butter or vegetable oil

APPLES AND RED CABBAGE INGREDIENTS

6 pieces smoked bacon, finely diced

1 medium onion, finely diced

1/4 cup (59 ml) cider vinegar

1 tablespoon honey

1/4 cup (55 g) light brown sugar

1 cup (237 ml) apple juice

1 cup (237 ml) Apple and Leek Stock or chicken stock

1 tablespoon caraway seeds

1 head savoy cabbage, shredded

1 head red cabbage, shredded

2 cooking apples, grated

METHOD

■ In a heavy skillet, brown the ground sausage over medium heat. Pour off the excess fat, add the celery, fennel, apple, and onion, and cook for 5 minutes over low heat to soften the vegetables. Season with salt and pepper. Remove from the heat, and add the bread crumbs. Then moisten the mixture with the cider, and set aside.

■ Preheat the oven to 450°F (232°C). Stuff and roll the roast, and tie the roll together with butcher's twine.

■ Mix the spices together. Rub the roast with oil, coat with the spice mixture, and place in a roasting pan. Place in the oven, turning the oven setting down to 350°F (177°C) right away. Roast for 30 minutes per pound (454 g) or about 1-1/2 hours. About 1/2 hour before the roast is done, rub the slices of baked potato with the softened butter or vegetable oil, spread them on a baking pan, and place the pan in the oven with the roast. Turn the potato slices over once during cooking.

■ Remove the roast from the oven when its internal temperature reaches 185°F (85°C). Also remove the potatoes. Allow the roast to rest for 20 minutes before slicing it.

■ To prepare the apples and red cabbage, first cook the bacon for 3 or 4 minutes over medium heat to render the fat. Add the onion, and sauté for about 3 minutes until the onion is soft and clear. Pour off the bacon fat.

■ Combine the vinegar and honey. Add this mixture, and the sugar, apple juice, stock, and caraway seeds to the bacon and onions, and bring to a boil.

■ Reduce the heat to a simmer. Add the cabbage and apples, cover tightly with aluminum foil, and braise for 45 minutes, until the cabbage is tender. Remove and keep warm until ready to serve.

■ Serve the sliced roulade with the apples and cabbage, and garnish with roasted potatoes.

Notes: Have your butcher cut a pocket in the pork loin or shoulder to hold the stuffing.

Prepare the apples and red cabbage, which take over an hour to complete, as the roast is cooking.

CIDER-GLAZED FILET *of* BEEF *on a* CRISPY APPLE, SCALLION, *and* NOODLE CAKE

Today's modern chefs often extend their search for culinary inspiration far beyond their own native lands. The crispy noodle cakes—an Asian element in this dish—are made with a very thin Italian spaghetti called capelli d'angelo or angel's hair.

Yields
6 SERVINGS

Apple Cider Reduction
(PAGE 132)

Apple and Leek Stock
(OPTIONAL: PAGE 134)

HAVE ON HAND

Tongs

NOODLE CAKE INGREDIENTS

2 eggs

1 pound (454 g) angel-hair pasta,
cooked, rinsed, and tossed with
1 tablespoon olive oil

1/2 teaspoon salt

1/4 teaspoon black pepper

6 scallions, white part only,
cut into thin circles

1 tart eating apple, peeled, cored, grated,
and tossed with 1 tablespoon lemon juice

2 tablespoons light cooking oil

STUFFING, GLAZED FILET, AND SAUCE INGREDIENTS

6 five-ounce (142 g) pieces of center-cut
filet mignon, 1" (2.5 cm) thick
(see "Notes")

3 tablespoons butter

2 tart eating apples, peeled, cored,
and cut into 1/4" (6 mm) cubes

2 scallions, white part only,
cut into thin circles

2 tablespoons light cooking oil

1/8 teaspoon black pepper

1/4 teaspoon cayenne pepper

6 tablespoons Apple Cider Reduction

1/2 cup (118 ml) Apple and Leek Stock,
beef stock, or chicken stock

1/4 teaspoon salt

■ Preheat the oven to 350°F (177°C).

■ Beat the eggs lightly, and toss them with the pasta, seasonings, scallions, and apple cubes. Divide this mixture into 6 equal portions. Heat the cooking oil in a sauté pan, and drop in 1 portion of the noodle mixture. With a pair of tongs, twist the noodles to form a pancake shape. In 3 to 4 minutes, the noodles will become brown and crispy. Turn the pancake over, and sauté the other side. Remove to a plate. Repeat this process to make a total of 6 noodle cakes. Trim any loose ends, and set aside until ready to use.

■ To begin the stuffing, heat the butter in a small saucepan over medium heat. When the butter sizzles, add the apple cubes and sliced scallions. Sauté for 4 minutes or until soft, tossing twice to prevent sticking. Remove from the heat, and keep warm on the back of the stove.

■ Next, preheat a heavy skillet over medium-high heat. Pat the meat dry. Add the cooking oil to the heated pan. Season the meat on both sides with one-half the black pepper, and add the meat to the pan. Sauté on one side for 4 to 5 minutes, or until well browned.

■ While the first side of the meat is cooking, place the noodle cakes in the preheated oven to warm. Also mix the cayenne pepper with the apple cider reduction.

■ Turn the meat over, and brush the cooked side with 2 tablespoons of the cider reduction. Cook the meat for another 4 to 5 minutes. (The meat will now be medium rare. For medium meat, add another 1-1/2 to 2 minutes per side.) When the meat is well browned, remove it from the pan, and place it on a large plate. Allow it to rest for 2 to 3 minutes, while you prepare the sauce.

■ Carefully discard the remaining hot fat, and wipe the skillet clean with a paper towel. Place the skillet back on the stove. Add the stock, remaining cider glaze, salt, and remaining black pepper.

■ Place the reheated noodle cakes on 6 individual serving dishes. With the point of a sharp knife, cut a small pocket in the middle of each filet, and fill each one with 2 tablespoons of the apple/scallion stuffing. Place a stuffed filet on top of each cake, divide the remaining stuffing among the plates, and drizzle with the cider sauce. Serve immediately.

Notes: The noodle cakes may be prepared up to 1 day in advance. To store them, wrap tightly with plastic food wrap, and refrigerate.

Take the meat out of the refrigerator about 30 minutes before cooking it.

LOIN of VENISON with an APPLE and DRIED CHERRY CRUST

Every fall I receive a piece of wild venison—a wonderful meat—from Nick, my fishmonger. Nick is a big man, and the image of him perched in a tree top, waiting to make his shot, amuses me. One note of caution: Venison is very lean, so it's easy to overcook. Mind your oven well.

Yields
8 TO 10 SERVINGS

Baking or silicone paper

Meat thermometer

4-quart (3.8 l) saucepan

INGREDIENTS

*4 pounds (1.8 kg) loin of venison,
trimmed of all connective tissue*

*1/4 pound (113 g) caul fat
(see "Notes")*

*3/4 cup (40 g) sun-dried cherries
or cranberries*

1/2 cup (118 ml) port wine

1/2 cup (118 ml) dry red wine

1 tablespoon chopped, fresh thyme

2 juniper berries, crushed

4 tart apples, peeled, cored, and sliced

1/2 teaspoon cumin

1/2 teaspoon coriander

1/4 teaspoon allspice

1/2 teaspoon salt

1/4 teaspoon black pepper

1 cup (100 g) fine bread crumbs

SWISS CHARD INGREDIENTS

*3 bunches Swiss chard, stem and ribs
removed, washed but not dried*

2 tablespoons water

2 tablespoons light cooking oil

Salt and pepper to taste

METHOD

■ Combine the sun-dried cherries, port wine, red wine, thyme, and juniper berries in a saucepan. Allow to soak for 30 minutes. Then place over medium heat, bring to a simmer, and simmer for 10 minutes, until the cherries are soft. Drain the cherries, and set them aside. Reserve the juice to use as a sauce for the venison.

■ In a second saucepan, combine the apples, cumin, coriander, and allspice.

Place the pan over low heat, and cook the apples for about 30 minutes, until they turn into a sauce. Be sure to stir them once every 5 minutes during cooking. Then add the drained cherries to the apple mixture, and cook for 5 more minutes over low heat. Remove from the heat, and allow to cool.

■ Purée the apples and cherries in a blender or a food processor. Season with the salt and pepper. Transfer the purée to a bowl, and blend in the bread crumbs.

■ Preheat the oven to 400°F (205°C). Place a sheet of baking paper on a flat surface, and spread out the caul fat on it. Spread the apple-cherry mixture in a 1/4"-thick (6 mm) layer over the fat, leaving about 2" (5.1 cm) around every edge free of purée.

■ Using the edge of the baking paper and starting at one end of the loin (as opposed to one long side), lift up the fat, and fold it over onto the loin. Peel away that portion of the paper, and let it hang free. Repeat with the opposite end of the paper. Then lift the sides of the paper, one by one, and fold them over the loin, which should now be completely encased in the apple-cherry crust and covered by the caul fat.

■ Use the baking paper to transfer the wrapped loin to a shallow roasting pan fitted with a rack or slotted pan. Roast to medium-rare, about 40 minutes. Use a meat thermometer to check the temperature after 20 minutes and every 5 minutes thereafter. For rare meat, the internal temperature should reach 130°F (54°C). Avoid internal temperatures of over 145°F (63°C).

■ Remove the loin from the oven, and allow it to rest about 10 minutes before slicing. As you wait, prepare the chard. Place 2 tablespoons of water in a 4-quart (3.8 l) saucepan over medium heat. When steam begins to rise from the pan, add the chard and toss continuously until the greens have wilted. Remove from the pot, and discard any remaining water.

■ Return the pan to the stove, and add the cooking oil. Quickly sauté the chard for no more than 1-1/2 minutes, seasoning it with the salt and pepper.

■ Place the loin on a serving platter, arrange the chard around it, and serve with the reserved cooking liquid from the cherries.

Notes: Caul fat, which you can order from many butchers, especially those who specialize in making sausages, is the lower stomach lining of a cow or pig. This thin, lacy membrane, with veins of fat running through it, melts and falls away during cooking, but while it's wrapped over a crust, it holds the crust in place and keeps meats and fillings moist and in place.

If you're unable to obtain caul fat, stuff the venison loin instead, by following the directions provided with the Turkey Roulade recipe on pages 58–59. Instead of flattening out the loin, as you would do with the turkey meat, use a sharp knife to cut the loin almost in half alongs its length, leaving one edge of the meat uncut to act as a hinge. Place the stuffing in the middle, and tie the loin back together with butcher's twine or cotton string.

When the caul fat is spread out (see "Method"), it should be 4 times as wide and 6" (15.2 cm) longer than the venison loin. If, for example, the loin is 4" (10.2 cm) wide and 10" (25.4 cm) long, the caul fat should cover an area 16" (40.6 cm) wide and 16" (40.6 cm) long. Piece the fat together if necessary.

As caul fat is very perishable, keep out only what you need. Wrap the remainder well, freeze it, and thaw it out under cold running water.

CIDER-CURED COUNTRY HAM

Someone once defined eternity as a ham and two people. When I first moved to the mountains of North Carolina, the salt-cured country ham I sampled there always struck me as too salty. As I later learned while working in the south of France, there is no bad food—only bad cooking. Now that I've discovered a better way to cook country ham, it finds its way into many of my menus. The keys to this recipe are scrubbing the ham and soaking it in cider for 24 hours.

Yields
30 SERVINGS

Apple Cider Reduction
(PAGE 132)

Apple Horseradish Sauce
(PAGES 94–95)

HAVE ON HAND

Bucket or plastic container
larger than the ham

Room in your refrigerator for the bucket!

6- to 8-gallon (22.7 to 30.3 l) stockpot
or roasting pan

Meat thermometer

INGREDIENTS

9 pound (4 kg) country ham, bone in and
outer layer of fat removed
(see "Notes")

2 gallons (7.6 l) fresh apple cider

1 tablespoon black pepper

1 cup (237 ml) very thick
Apple Cider Reduction

2 bay leaves

30 whole cloves

METHOD

■ Rinse the ham under cold running water, scrubbing its entire outer surface with a stiff vegetable brush. Place the ham in a bucket or plastic container just big enough to hold it. Pour in the cider, and refrigerate for 24 hours.

■ The next day, skim any fat that has risen to the surface of the cider. Place the ham in a large stockpot or in a roasting pan just large enough to hold it. Pour the cider over the ham, place over medium heat, and bring to a boil. Then lower the heat and simmer the ham for 3 hours (allow 20 minutes per pound or 454 g) or until the internal temperature reaches 150°F (51°C). Turn the ham if necessary.

■ Preheat the oven to 350°F (177°C). Transfer the ham from the pot to a roasting pan fitted with a rack. Discard the cider, which will be too salty for any other use. Add the pepper to the thick apple cider reduction, and brush the reduction onto the surface of the ham. Stick the whole cloves into the ham, spacing them evenly. Roast for about 2 hours, until a nice, dark crust has developed and the meat is tender. The internal temperature of the ham should reach 165°F (74°C).

■ Slice the ham very thinly, and serve with Apple Horseradish Sauce. When you've finished cutting the meat off the bone, use the bone to make a soup.

Notes: There are two ways to salt hams: brining and dry-curing. What I call country ham here is the dry-cured variety.

The ham may be prepared a few days in advance, as it is excellent either hot or cold.

PORK TENDERLOIN
SERVED *in the* STYLE *of a* GOOD HOUSEWIFE

This recipe has its roots in a cookbook written in 1587 for "The Good Husvvifes Ievvell." The original recipe calls for rabbit, but roast turkey, duck, goose, or pork all work well. The style of service, in which bread serves as the base, traces its origins to a time when there were no plates and food was served on top of "tranche"—thick slices of bread.

Yields
8 MAIN-COURSE SERVINGS OR 12 BUFFET SERVINGS

BASIC RECIPE INCLUDED

Apple Cider Reduction
(PAGE 132)

Ovenproof serving dish

ROAST PORK INGREDIENTS

3 ten- to twelve-ounce (284 to 340 g)
pork tenderloins,
silver skin membrane removed

1 teaspoon mace

1 teaspoon allspice

1/2 teaspoon cumin

1/4 teaspoon nutmeg

1/4 teaspoon salt

1/2 teaspoon black pepper

1 tablespoon light cooking oil

SAUCE AND GARNISH INGREDIENTS

4 tablespoons butter

2 small red onions, peeled and thinly sliced

3 cooking apples, peeled, cored, and sliced

2 cups (473 ml) dry red wine

2 tablespoons cider vinegar

2 tablespoons Apple Cider Reduction

1 tablespoon honey

1/2 teaspoon salt

1/2 teaspoon black pepper

1/2 teaspoon mace

1/2 teaspoon allspice

1/2 teaspoon nutmeg

1/8 teaspoon cloves

1 teaspoon peeled, minced, fresh ginger

1 tablespoon fresh lemon grass
(or lemon zest)

3 cups (300 g) lightly toasted bread cubes

2 eating apples, sliced

■ Preheat the oven to 425°F (218°C). Combine the spices, salt, and pepper. Rub the cooking oil over the surface of the pork. Dry your hands, and coat the pork with the spice mixture. Place the tenderloins in a shallow roasting pan, and roast for 25 minutes. Remove the pork from the oven, and set aside. Turn the oven down to 350°F (177°C).

■ To begin the sauce, melt the butter and sauté the onions for 3 minutes in a heavy skillet over medium-high heat. Add the apples, and continue to cook for another 4 to 5 minutes, until the onions are transparent. Add all of the remaining ingredients except the bread. Turn the heat down to medium-low, and cook for 5 minutes.

■ Spread the bread out in an ovenproof dish, and pour the sauce over the top. Slice each tenderloin into 12 pieces, and arrange on top. Reheat in the oven for 5 minutes. Before serving, garnish with slices of fresh apple.

Mrs. Clark, my fifth-grade teacher at Palm Cove Beach School, once made baked beans for a class picnic. I will never forget them. They were creamy in texture—neither too dry nor too watery—and had the deep, rich flavor that results from the perfect marriage of individual flavors into a glorious whole. I've never been able to duplicate Mrs. Clark's beans, but I think that this recipe is almost as unforgettable.

Yields
8 SERVINGS

3 cups (525 g) dried white navy beans

1 small onion, diced

6 tablespoons molasses

1/4 cup (59 ml) Dijon mustard

2 tablespoons tomato paste

2 teaspoons salt

1 tablespoon black pepper

2 sprigs fresh thyme

1 bay leaf

2 teaspoons cider vinegar

2 tablespoons soy sauce

2 cups (473 ml) fresh apple cider, boiling

1/2 cup (118 ml) bourbon

■ Rinse the beans, picking out any stones or other foreign objects. Place in a pot with enough cold water to cover, and bring to a boil over medium heat. Drain and rinse the beans, and return to the pot, again with enough cold water to cover. Bring to a boil. Then reduce the heat, and simmer for 30 minutes, skimming and discarding any foam that rises to the top. Drain the beans well.

■ Preheat the oven to 250°F (121°C). Place the beans in an ovenproof casserole. Add all the remaining ingredients except the bourbon, and pour in enough boiling water to cover the beans. Cover the casserole with a lid or foil, and bake for 6 to 9 hours, adding a little water if necessary. Several minutes before the beans are fully cooked, add the bourbon.

Apples AND Your Health

An apple a day really can help keep the doctor away. In fact, apples are one of the most nutritious foods around. With only 80 calories per medium apple, they have almost no fat and are cholesterol and sodium free. Apples also contain essential nutrients,

such as potassium, thiamine, riboflavin, phosphorus, magnesium, iron, and vitamins A and C. They are high in complex carbohydrates and contain the trace mineral, boron. New research suggests that flavonoids—naturally occurring chemicals found in apples—may reduce the risk of heart disease and inhibit the development of certain cancers.

Evidence indicates that eating apples can also help reduce levels of serum cholesterol, which in turn helps reduce the risk of heart attacks caused by coronary heart disease. A medium apple has approximately 4 grams of fiber of which about 80 percent is water-soluble fiber or pectin—credited with helping to lower cholesterol. The remaining 20 percent of the fiber in apples is insoluble and is thought to aid in preventing cancer.

The apple is particularly helpful to diabetics, as it contains fruit sugar (fructose) and provides a quick, healthy snack. Fruit sugar does not cause a rapid rise in blood sugar and keeps blood sugar glucose levels consistently high.

ROASTED CAPON *with* APPLE BUTTER

Placing a stuffing between the skin and meat of a capon results in an especially flavorful and juicy roast. Roasting times for these birds will vary. Plan on about 20 minutes per pound (454 g), but check periodically by pricking the joint between the leg and the thigh. If the juices run clear, the meat is done. If the juices are still pink, keep on cooking. If no juice appears, march out and shoot yourself—you've overcooked your capon. A meat thermometer will make overcooking—and your demise—less likely.

Yields
8 MAIN-COURSE SERVINGS OR 12 BUFFET SERVINGS

BASIC AND ADDITIONAL
RECIPES INCLUDED

Apple Butter
(PAGE 135)

Swiss Chard and Spinach
(PAGE 99)

Susie's Applesauce
(PAGE 87)

Butcher's twine or cotton string

Meat thermometer

INGREDIENTS

1 six-pound (2.7 kg) capon

1-1/2 cups (355 ml) Apple Butter

1 tablespoon chopped, fresh thyme

1/2 teaspoon salt

1/2 teaspoon black pepper

2 tablespoons olive oil flavored with
1 teaspoon lemon zest

■ Preheat the oven to 450°F (232°C). Wash the capon inside and out, and pat dry. Starting at the breast bone and using your fingers, slowly work the skin free from the meat. Work as far into the chicken as you can, even loosening the skin around the legs if possible.

■ Mix together the apple butter, thyme, salt, and pepper. Again using your fingers, spread a thin layer of this mixture between the skin and meat. You'll find this easiest if you start with the deepest sections and work your way out.

■ Press the capon skin back into contact with the meat, and press the bird back into a compact shape. Use the butcher's twine to tie the legs and wings securely. Rub the capon with the lemon-flavored olive oil, and place on a greased rack in a roasting pan.

■ Place the bird in the oven, and immediately turn the heat down to 350°F (177°C). After 20 minutes, begin basting the capon every 10 minutes, using the drippings in the roasting pan. Allow about 2 hours cooking time, but start checking for doneness after the first hour.

■ Remove from the oven when done. Remove the twine, slice the meat, and serve with Susie's Applesauce (page 87) and Swiss Chard and Spinach (page 99).

HEAVEN-*and*-EARTH *with* CHICKEN-*and*-APPLE SAUSAGE

Although sausages have disappeared from many kitchens, due largely to our interest in better health, they still have a place in our menus, especially now that chefs have discovered ways to make them leaner. In this sausage recipe, I've borrowed a technique from my teacher, Madeleine Kamman, who substitutes a few eggs and a little more lean meat to her sausage to make it lighter. One hint: If you find that small sausage casings are hard to come by, just shape the sausage mixture into patties.

The traditional German recipe, Heaven-and-Earth, is combined here with grilled sausages and Apple Cider Reduction, but can also be served as a separate vegetable course.

Yields
6 SERVINGS

BASIC RECIPES INCLUDED
___

Applesauce
(PAGE 135)

Apple Cider Reduction
(PAGE 132)

*Meat grinder with medium
and fine grinding blades*

*Sausage tube for the grinder,
or a sausage press*

Slotted spoon

SAUSAGE INGREDIENTS

*1 pound (454 g) chicken,
bones and skin removed*

1 cup (237 ml) Applesauce

1/3 pound (151 g) fresh, unsalted fatback

3 tablespoons dry sherry

1/4 teaspoon cloves

1/4 teaspoon cinnamon

1/4 teaspoon ginger

1/4 teaspoon coriander

1 tablespoon salt

1-1/4 teaspoons black pepper

1 teaspoon chopped, fresh sage leaves

7 eggs

1 large onion, peeled

2 shallots, peeled

Small sausage casing

Additional salt, pepper, and sage to taste

Apple Cider Reduction

HEAVEN-AND-EARTH AND GARNISH INGREDIENTS

4 medium potatoes, peeled

3 cooking apples, peeled and cored

*6 slices smoked bacon (rind removed)
or pancetta*

2 teaspoons salt

1 teaspoon white pepper

3 tablespoons chopped, fresh parsley

Red cabbage, several uncooked slices

■ Using a meat grinder with a medium blade, mix and grind the chicken, applesauce, fatback, sherry, spices, salt, pepper, sage, and eggs. Divide the ground forcemeat in half, and, using a fine grinding blade, grind one-half of the mixture twice. Mix the two halves together by combining them and putting them through the grinder once again.

■ Run the onion and shallots through the grinder, and mix them into the forcemeat by hand. Using either a sausage press or a sausage tube on your grinder, fill the sausage casing with forcemeat, twisting it to make links that are each about 5" (12.7 cm) long.

■ To cook the sausages, preheat a heavy skillet over medium heat, cut the links apart, and sauté them for about 10 minutes or until golden on all sides. Season with salt, pepper, and sage, and keep warm until ready to serve.

■ To prepare the Heaven-and-Earth, first cut the potatoes into large cubes, and boil in salted water until tender, about 15 minutes. Drain thoroughly. Cut the apples into 1/4" (6 mm) pieces, and set aside.

■ Preheat a heavy skillet (I use one for all my sauté work) over medium-low heat. Add the bacon, and cook until crispy. With a slotted spoon, remove the bacon, leaving the rendered fat in the skillet. Drain the bacon on a paper towel, and reserve.

■ Place the apples and potatoes in the skillet, and cook over medium heat, stirring frequently. Add the bacon, and continue to cook until the apples are tender and the potatoes are slightly browned. Remove from the pan, add the salt and white pepper, mix together, and toss with parsley.

■ Serve with the sausages, garnishing each dish with several slices of fresh red cabbage, and offering the apple cider reduction on the side.

Note: If you don't plan to cook the sausages you make within 24 hours, freeze or poach them for future use. To poach them, select a stainless steel cooking vessel that is large enough to hold them in a single layer. Fill the pot half full with liquid. (Cider, water, a flavored broth called Court Bouillon, fish or chicken stock, or the Apple and Leek Stock on page 134 may be used as the cooking liquid.) Bring the liquid to a boil, then reduce the heat, add the sausages, and allow them to simmer for 20 minutes. Remove from the liquid, drain, and cool. If they're refrigerated, the poached sausages will now keep for up to 1 week. (If you've used cider as your poaching liquid, strain it through a cheesecloth, and use it for making stock.)

APPLE RATATOUILLE

This recipe makes an excellent side dish for grilled meats or fish, but can also be served by itself as a cold or warm salad. I like to cook the ingredients separately and then combine them for a final seasoning and blending.

Yields
3 CUPS (710 ML)

1/4 cup (59 ml) walnut oil

1/4 cup (59 ml) light cooking oil

1 crisp eating apple, peeled, cored, and diced

1 small red onion, peeled and diced

2 small zucchini, diced

1 small yellow squash, diced

2 cloves garlic, peeled and finely diced

1 tomato, blanched, peeled, seeded, and diced

1/4 cup (60 g) English walnuts

1 teaspoon salt

1/2 teaspoon black pepper

1/4 teaspoon nutmeg

1/4 teaspoon turmeric

12 fresh basil leaves

Apple slices, fresh basil, and spinach leaves

■ Add one-half of each oil to a heavy skillet placed over medium heat. Sauté the diced apple, onion, zucchini, and squash—one at a time—until golden brown, adding additional oil as necessary for each batch. Remove each batch when it's done.

■ Next, sauté the garlic for 2 minutes. Then return the apples and vegetables to the skillet, and add the tomato, walnuts, salt, pepper, nutmeg, and turmeric as the ratatouille continues to cook.

■ Cut the 12 basil leaves into thin ribbons, and add them to the ratatouille right away. (If you cut the basil too soon, it will turn black.) Turn the heat off, and allow the ratatouille to cool.

■ Either rewarm and serve with grilled meats or fish, or serve cold as a salad garnished with apple slices, fresh basil, and spinach leaves.

CREAMY POLENTA *with* SAUTÉED APPLES

Polenta, grits, gnocchi, and mashed potatoes are all making comebacks as "comfort" foods. Why? Because they taste good and they're filling, too—which is why we eat, right? Treat yourself and your friends to this dish. You deserve it.

Yields
6 TO 8 SERVINGS

BASIC RECIPE INCLUDED

Apple and Leek Stock
(OPTIONAL; PAGE 134)

INGREDIENTS

3 cups (710 ml) water or stock

1 cup (237 ml) fresh apple cider

1 teaspoon salt

*1 cup (170 g) uncooked fine polenta
or grits (see "Notes")*

*4 tablespoons (20 g) freshly grated
Parmesan cheese*

2 tablespoons butter

*2 cooking apples, peeled, cored, and cut
into 1/2" (1.3 cm) cubes*

Several tablespoons heavy cream (optional)

Slivers of unpeeled green apple

METHOD

■ You'll be cooking the polenta and apples separately but simultaneously, so be sure to prepare all the ingredients in advance.

■ Bring the water (or stock), cider, and salt to a rolling boil. Sprinkle the polenta slowly into the liquid, stirring continuously with a wire whisk until all the polenta has been incorporated. Turn the heat down to low, and continue to stir the polenta as it cooks for 10 to 15 minutes more. Check the seasoning, and then add the cheese and the butter, and mix in vigorously.

■ As the polenta is cooking, cook the apple cubes in a saucepan over low heat until they're just tender and are starting to fall apart. Add them to the polenta during the last 2 to 3 minutes of cooking.

■ Serve immediately. If you like, mix a few tablespoons of cream into the finished dish, and garnish with apple slivers to add appetizing color.

Notes: When I'm eating this dish, 6 servings become one!

The basic cooking ratio for polenta is 4 cups of liquid to 1 cup of polenta. In this recipe, Apple and Leek Stock or other stocks can be substituted for the water.

ESPALIER APPLE TREE (BROCADED WEAVING)   LAURA FOSTER NICHOLSON

SPRING LETTUCES *with*
CIDER ALMOND SWEET *and* SOUR DRESSING

For simplicity, nothing replaces a well-prepared salad made with garden fresh lettuces. This cider dressing, which can be made in advance and refrigerated for weeks, was the standard dressing at my restaurant for many years. Remember to mix it thoroughly before serving.

Yields

6 SALADS AND 3 CUPS (710 ML) DRESSING

INGREDIENTS

1-1/4 cups (150 g) blanched almonds

10 tablespoons light salad oil

10 tablespoons fresh apple cider

1/2 cup (118 ml) cider vinegar

6 tablespoons honey

Baby bibb lettuce, 2 small heads

Baby romaine, 1 small head

Red oak-leaf lettuce, 1 small head

Croutons

METHOD

■ Combine the first 5 ingredients in a bowl. Using a blender, purée them in batches until smooth. Refrigerate.

■ Pick and wash the lettuces, and pat dry. Just before serving, toss with the dressing and garnish with croutons.

SUSIE'S APPLESAUCE

I love this recipe, which comes from my friend in Kansas, Susie Herynk Huffman. The beautifully pink, cinnamon-flavored applesauce is a great variation on an already wonderful theme and can be frozen to a slushy consistency and served with warm pie or included in ham sandwiches. When Susie makes her applesauce, she uses Green Transparents.

Yields
1 QUART (.9 L)

BASIC RECIPE INCLUDED	METHOD
Applesauce (PAGE 135)	■ Combine all the ingredients in a saucepan, and place over low heat. Cook, stirring frequently, for about 30 minutes or until the candy has dissolved. Remove from the heat, and allow to cool before serving.

INGREDIENTS

4 cups (.9 l) Applesauce

1 three-ounce (85 g) package of clear cinnamon candy

1/4 cup (59 ml) fresh apple cider

SMOKED CORN *and* APPLE SOUP

This recipe has a few variations, each with a slightly different and distinctive flavor. If you don't have access to a charcoal smoker, either grill the corn on a charcoal grill or roast it in the oven. You may also smoke or roast the apples.

Yields
6 SERVINGS

Apple and Leek Stock
(OPTIONAL; PAGE 134)

HAVE ON HAND

*Charcoal smoker, charcoal grill,
or baking sheet*

INGREDIENTS

*6 ears sweet corn
(see "Notes")*

2 tart cooking apples

2 large potatoes

2 leeks, white part only

*8 cups (1.9 l) Apple and Leek Stock
or chicken stock*

1/2 teaspoon cayenne

2 teaspoons salt

1/2 teaspoon cumin

4 sprigs fresh thyme leaves

2 scallions, thinly sliced

12 slices French bread, grilled or toasted

Cream or crème fraîche (optional)

■ Shuck the corn, remove all the silk, and rinse. Prepare the smoker, and smoke the corn for 30 minutes. If you choose to smoke the apples, too, leave them whole, and do so at the same time; they will also require 30 minutes in the smoker.

■ To grill the corn instead, brush the ears with 2 tablespoons of light cooking oil, and place on your charcoal grill. Depending on how hot the coals are (medium heat is best), the corn should be grilled for about 10 minutes or until it is golden in color.

■ Roasting the corn is also possible. Brush with 2 tablespoons of light cooking oil, and place on a baking sheet. Roast for 20 minutes in an oven preheated to 400°F (205°C), turning once after 10 minutes. (The apples may be roasted at the same time and in the same manner, but cut them in half first and don't brush them with oil.)

■ Cut the cooked corn from the cob. Peel and core the apples, and cut them into chunks. Peel the potatoes, and cut into pieces that are equal in size to the apple chunks. Remove and discard the tough outer layer of each leek, rinse thoroughly, and cut the leeks into 1/2"-thick (1.3 cm) slices.

■ Bring the stock to a boil in the stockpot, and continue to boil until the volume has been reduced by one-third. Add the vegetables and apples while the stock is boiling, and then turn the heat down to a simmer. Add the cayenne, salt, cumin, and thyme, and continue to simmer the soup for 1 hour. Test the potatoes and leeks to make sure they're tender. When they are, remove the soup from the heat, and allow it to cool. Purée the soup in a blender, checking the seasoning as you do.

■ To serve, reheat the soup, garnish with scallions, and serve with slices of grilled or toasted French bread. This soup may also be served cold with a little cream or crème fraîche. (Crème fraîche is a slightly soured cream, halfway between fresh heavy cream and sour cream in texture.)

Notes: If you choose to grill or roast the corn, add 2 tablespoons of light cooking oil to your list of ingredients.

For additional flavor, add the corn cobs to your stock.

MARINATED *and* GRILLED APPLE *and* RED ONION SALAD

Serve this salad warm or cold, depending on the weather and your mood. Both tangy and sweet in flavor, it's bound to lift your spirits.

Yields
6 SERVINGS

BASIC RECIPE INCLUDED

Cider Verjus
(PAGE 133)

1/2 cup (118 ml) walnut oil

1/2 cup (118 ml) light salad oil

1/2 cup (118 ml) Cider Verjus

2 tablespoons Dijon mustard

1 teaspoon salt

1/2 teaspoon black pepper

2 small red onions, peeled

2 eating apples

1 tablespoon light cooking oil

1 head romaine lettuce

1 apple, thinly sliced (optional)

■ To make the dressing, first whisk the two oils together in a mixing bowl. Then add the verjus, mustard, salt, and pepper. Whisk lightly, just enough to blend the ingredients. Set aside.

■ Slice the onions into thin circles and the apples into 1/4"-thick (6 mm) rings. Place in a mixing bowl, toss with 4 tablespoons of the dressing, and marinate for 30 minutes before grilling.

■ Pick and discard the tough, outer leaves of the romaine, and cut the remaining leaves into 1/4"-wide (6 mm) ribbons. Place in a large mixing bowl, cover with a damp tea towel or paper towel, and refrigerate until ready to use.

■ Lightly oil the grill. Drain the onions and apples, and grill them over medium-low heat for 2 minutes on each side; they should retain some of their crispness. To create attractive grill marks on them, rotate them 90°, once on each side.

■ If you'd like to serve this salad warm, toss the romaine with 1/3 to 1/2 cup (79 to 118 ml) of the dressing while you're grilling the onions and apples. Arrange the lettuce on 6 serving plates. Move the grilled onions and apples to a plate, and allow them to cool for 3 or 4 minutes. Then arrange them on the salad plates, and drizzle 1 tablespoon of additional dressing over each serving.

■ If you'd rather serve this salad cold, place the grilled onions and apples in a mixing bowl, toss with 6 tablespoons of dressing, and refrigerate until cool. When you're ready to serve the salad, toss the lettuce with the dressing, and arrange on individual plates. Drain the onions and apples if necessary, and arrange them around the lettuce. Garnish the cold salad with thin slices of fresh apple.

Notes: Allow 1 hour for preparation, as the onions and apples must be marinated.

Use a stainless steel knife when cutting the lettuce, as a carbon blade will discolor it. When slicing the romaine, cut perpendicular to the ribs on the leaves.

Boys Apples buy . Jocky looks shy

Apple, Leek, and Potato Soup

This is a variation on the classic French vichyssoise—a leek and onion soup that is usually served cold. There are two ways to prepare this dish: puréed and strained, or not. The latter method may be less elegant, but the results taste just as good.

Yields
6 SERVINGS

Apple and Leek Stock
(OPTIONAL; PAGE 134)

INGREDIENTS

2 tablespoons butter

4 leeks, white portions only,
cut in thin circles

1 medium onion, peeled and thinly sliced

4 large potatoes, peeled and cut into
1/2" (1.3 cm) cubes

2 cooking apples, peeled and cut
into 1/2" (1.3 cm) cubes

4 cups (946 ml) Apple and Leek Stock
or chicken stock

1 cup (237 ml) water

1 cup (237 ml) fresh apple cider

2 teaspoons salt

1 cup (237 ml) half-and-half

METHOD

■ Melt the butter in a stockpot over medium-low heat. Add the leeks and onion slices, and toss. Cover and allow the vegetables to sweat until soft, but don't brown them; the soup should be light in color. Stir every few minutes to prevent sticking and burning.

■ When the onions and leeks are soft, add the potatoes, apples, stock, water, cider, and salt. Slowly bring the mixture to a simmer, and cook gently for 45 minutes or until the potatoes are soft.

■ At this point, either add the half-and-half, and serve the soup hot, or allow the soup to cool, add the half-and-half, and serve cold. To make the more elegant version, purée the cold soup in a blender or food processor, and pass it through a strainer. Try serving this superb dish with crusty French bread.

Note: To prepare the soup in advance, wait until just before serving to add the half-and-half, refrigerating or freezing the soup in the meantime.

APPLE HORSERADISH SAUCE

Along with coriander, nettle, horehound, and lettuce, horseradish is one of the five bitter herbs of the Passover celebration. Its pungent flavor goes well with dishes that include fatty meats. Turn to the recipe on pages 72–73 for an especially tempting example.

Yields
3/4 CUP (177 ML)

Applesauce
(PAGE 135)

INGREDIENTS

1/2 pound (227 g) fresh horseradish root

1 cup (237 ml) vinegar

1/2 teaspoon salt

1/4 cup (59 ml) Applesauce

2 tablespoons heavy cream

1/4 teaspoon allspice

1/8 teaspoon nutmeg

METHOD

■ Wash the horseradish root in hot water, scrubbing it well with a stiff vegetable brush. Combine the vinegar and salt in a glass or stainless steel bowl. Scrape the skin from the root, and discard. Grate or mince the horseradish into the vinegar. (To store this mixture, pack into sterile jars, seal, and keep in a cool place.)

■ Combine 1/2 cup (118 ml) of the fresh horseradish preparation with the rest of the ingredients, and mix well.

Note: While this recipe calls for fresh horseradish root, you can certainly substitute the dried, ground version. Combine 1 tablespoon of dried, ground horseradish with 1 tablespoon of water. After letting the mixture rest for 30 minutes, mix in 1/2 cup (118 ml) of heavy cream. Substitute this mixture for the 1/2 cup of fresh horseradish preparation called for in the "Method" section of this recipe, eliminating the extra 2 tablespoons of cream in the ingredients list.

Johnny APPLESEED

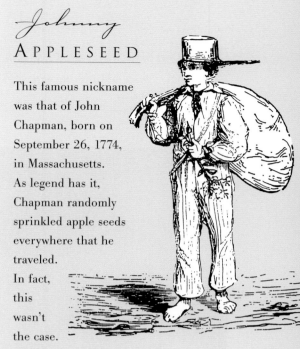

This famous nickname was that of John Chapman, born on September 26, 1774, in Massachusetts. As legend has it, Chapman randomly sprinkled apple seeds everywhere that he traveled. In fact, this wasn't the case. Chapman was well aware of the fact that apples grow better from seedlings than from seeds; he actually worked to develop nurseries filled with apple seedlings.

Chapman was a tall man whose search for land drove him first, at age twenty-three, into western Pennsylvania, where his goal was—what else?—to grow apples. Although he was constantly acquiring land, Chapman, who preferred to sleep outdoors, was often scantily dressed and never owned a house. He frequently went barefoot regardless of the season and sometimes wore a hat that doubled as a cooking pot.

As the frontier moved west, so did Chapman, and he spent the last forty years of his life traveling in that direction. Wherever he stopped, he would plant, sell, and give away apple trees and seeds before he moved on. Chapman was also a missionary of the Swedenborgian faith and spent a good deal of time handing out religious tracts and preaching.

Although the details of his life have been obscured by legend, his nickname and many of his apple trees still remain as testaments to John Chapman's love of apples.

APPLES *and* SAUERKRAUT

The health benefits of sauerkraut have been recorded since 200 B.C., when it was served to laborers working on the Great Wall of China. Cooking sauerkraut in cider, as is done in this recipe, mellows its strong flavor.

Yields
12 SERVINGS

INGREDIENTS

2 tablespoons bacon fat or light cooking oil

1/2 cup (80 g) peeled, thinly sliced shallots

1 quart (.9 l) drained sauerkraut

2 tart apples, peeled, cored, and sliced

2 cups (473 ml) fresh apple cider

4 juniper berries

METHOD

■ Preheat the oven to 325°F (163°C). In an ovenproof casserole, heat the bacon fat or oil over medium heat. Add the shallots, and sauté until transparent—about 3 minutes. Add the sauerkraut, sauté for 5 minutes, and then add the apple slices.

■ Bring the cider to a boil, and pour it into the casserole. Add the juniper berries, reduce the heat, and simmer, uncovered, for 30 minutes. Then cover with a lid or foil, and bake for 30 minutes. Remove and serve.

ANNA'S PEPPERED BEETS

Either you love beets or you don't; I happen to love their very earthy flavor. Anna's Beets are delicious served as a salad on a bed of greens or as a condiment for other dishes. This recipe is easy to prepare and can be served hot or cold.

Yields
6 SERVINGS

INGREDIENTS

6 baseball-sized beets

1 large or 2 small tart apples

2 tablespoons butter

1 teaspoon salt

1/2 teaspoon black pepper

1 small eating apple, peeled, cored, and cut into 1/2" (1.3 cm) cubes

12 sprigs fresh dill

1 teaspoon toasted sesame seeds

METHOD

■ Preheat the oven to 400°F (205°C). Place the unpeeled beets on a baking sheet, and roast for 1 hour, checking after 45 minutes by piercing with the point of a knife. When the beets are done, the knife point should sink easily to a depth of 1/2" (1.3 cm) and then hit the firm inner portion of the beet.

■ Remove the beets from the oven, and while they're cooling, peel, core, and cube the tart apples. Then peel the beets, and cut them into 1" (1.3 cm) cubes. Place in a saucepan along with the tart apples, butter, salt, and pepper. Cover the pan tightly, and place over low heat for 45 minutes, until the apples have cooked to a purée and the beets are soft. Remove from the pan, mash to a chunky consistency with a fork or a potato masher, and check the seasonings, adding more if desired.

■ To serve, divide the beets among 6 plates, sprinkle a few sesame seeds on top, add the cubes of eating apple, and arrange the dill sprigs around the sides.

BRAISED LEEKS, APPLES, and NAPA CABBAGE with SWEET SPICE

I'm always a little sad when fall comes around because the wealth of fresh summer vegetables begins to decline. Fortunately, some leafy green vegetables are still available in the autumn, and, by adding some leeks, a fine vegetable dish can be had.

The spice combination used here is called "sweet spice," and the proportions called for are Madeleine Kamman's. Sweet spice is something I never lack in my kitchen, as it plays an important role in many of the flavors I compose.

Yields
12 SERVINGS

4-quart (3.8 l) saucepan

SWEET SPICE INGREDIENTS

1 teaspoon cinnamon

2 teaspoons allspice

1/8 teaspoon cloves

1/2 teaspoon cardamom

1 teaspoon nutmeg

2 teaspoons coriander

LEEKS, APPLES, AND NAPA
CABBAGE INGREDIENTS

*2 large leeks, white part only,
cut into julienne*

3 tablespoons light cooking oil

1 head Napa cabbage, cut into chiffonade

2 tart apples, peeled, cored, and sliced

1/2 teaspoon salt

1/2 teaspoon black pepper

2 teaspoons Sweet Spice

SWISS CHARD AND SPINACH
INGREDIENTS

*3 bunches Swiss chard, stem and ribs
removed, washed but not dried*

*1 pound (454 g) spinach, stem and ribs
removed, washed but not dried*

3 tablespoons light cooking oil

1/2 teaspoon salt

1/2 teaspoon black pepper

2 teaspoons Sweet Spice

■ Mix together the sweet spice ingredients, and set aside. Warm a serving platter.

■ In a heavy skillet over medium heat, sauté the leeks in the cooking oil for 3 minutes. Add the Napa cabbage, cook for 4 minutes, and then add the apples, salt, pepper, and sweet spice. Cook for another 3 or 4 minutes, stirring frequently. Place on the warmed serving platter.

■ Place 2 tablespoons of water in a 4-quart (3.8 l) saucepan over medium heat. When steam begins to rise from the pan, add the chard and spinach, tossing continuously until the greens have wilted. Remove the greens from the pot, and discard any remaining water.

■ Return the pan to the stove, and add the cooking oil. Quickly sauté the greens for no more than 1-1/2 minutes, seasoning them with the salt, pepper, and sweet spice. Arrange on the warmed serving platter, and serve.

THE *Apple* OF *Whose Eye?*

Is biting into a Granny Smith and feeling your mouth pucker at its tartness a pleasure to you? Or would you rather enjoy the mellow taste of a sweet, juicy Gala? Our choice of a favorite apple is determined by strong personal and cultural preferences. Many Europeans, for example, savor an apple with a "crunch" to it—one that's crisp and slightly tart. In Japan, however, where very sweet apples are valued highly, the fruit is sometimes left to ripen until the core of the apple is almost syrupy—a condition that Europeans call "water core damage."

The perfect apple is always in the mind—and on the tongue—of the person who selects it. If you're planning an orchard, take the time to find and taste the apple varieties you want to grow before you plant the trees.

Three APPLE CANAPÉS

As with many of the recipes I've written, these three contain some "mini" recipes—components which I use over and over, such as the salsa in the fudge and the marinated lemons in the dip. The apple salsa is excellent served over grilled fish or chicken. The purée in the dip recipe can be used as a flavoring for baked fish, in salad dressing, or with cooked vegetables.

Notes: To some extent, all these canapés can be prepared in advance. The strudel, however, should be baked about 30 minutes before serving; baked phyllo tends to become limp when it sits too long.

The beans in the last recipe must be soaked overnight, and the marinated lemons must be prepared two days in advance.

APPLE, PANCETTA, and SCALLION STRUDEL

Yields
APPROXIMATELY 24 SMALL CANAPÉS

INGREDIENTS

3 cooking apples, peeled, cored, and chopped

1/2 cup (114 g) diced pancetta, smoked bacon, or prosciutto

6 scallions, cut into thin circles

1/2 teaspoon black pepper

6 tablespoons finely chopped parsley

1 egg white

4 sheets phyllo dough

6 tablespoons butter, melted

METHOD

■ In a saucepan over medium-low heat, sweat the apples until they become soft. While they're cooking, sauté the pancetta in a separate pan to render the fat and brown the meat lightly. Discard the fat when done.

■ Add the scallions to the pancetta, and cook for 1 minute. Then add this mixture to the cooked apples. Season with pepper, and add the parsley. Remove from the heat immediately, and allow to cool to room temperature.

■ Preheat the oven to 425°F (218°C). You'll now make 2 "logs," each consisting of 2 sheets of phyllo pastry. Start by beating the egg white lightly with a fork and blending it into the cooled apple mixture. Then, on a flat surface, lay out 2 sheets of phyllo pastry, side by side. Brush each sheet liberally with melted butter, top each sheet with a second sheet of phyllo, and brush the upper sheets with butter.

■ Divide the apple filling between the 2 layered sheets, spreading it along one edge of each piece of pastry. Roll the pastry into logs, brushing the pastry with butter as you do.

■ Place the 2 strudels on a buttered baking sheet. With a sharp knife, make 1/2"-long (1.3 cm) scores across the top of each roll; these "starter" cuts will make slicing the baked strudel easier. At this point, the strudel can be refrigerated for up to 24 hours.

■ Bake the strudels for approximately 20 minutes or until the dough is golden brown and flaky. Remove and let rest for 5 minutes; then slice and serve.

APPLE SALSA "FUDGE"

Yields
48 SMALL PIECES

HAVE ON HAND

9" x 12" (22.9 x 30.5 cm) baking dish

INGREDIENTS

2 tart eating apples, peeled, cored, and finely diced

1 medium red onion, peeled and finely diced

1/2 cucumber, peeled, seeded, and finely diced

2 jalapeño peppers, seeds removed and finely diced

2 tablespoons chopped parsley

4 tablespoons chopped cilantro

Juice of 2 limes

4 tablespoons olive oil

1/2 teaspoon salt

1 teaspoon black pepper

1 cup (229 g) salsa

1/2 pound (227 g) grated cheddar cheese

3 eggs, lightly beaten

1/2 pound (227 g) grated cheddar cheese

METHOD

■ Preheat the oven to 350°F (177°C), and grease the baking dish.

■ Blend together all the ingredients except for the second 1/2 pound (227 g) of grated cheese. Pour the mixture into the baking dish, top with the remaining cheese, and bake for 35 minutes or until the cheese is golden brown and the "fudge" has set.

■ Remove from the oven, and allow to cool for 5 minutes. Cut into 1-1/2" (2.5 cm) squares and serve.

Lemon Purée, Apple, and Navy Bean Dip

Yields
3 to 4 cups (710 to 946 ml)

Have on Hand

Small, lidded container

Blender or food processor

Marinated Lemon Purée Ingredients

3 lemons

2 tablespoons salt

2 tablespoons granulated sugar

2 cloves garlic, peeled and finely diced

1 teaspoon chopped marjoram leaves

3 tablespoons olive oil

Apple Bean Dip Ingredients

2 cups (524 g) dried white navy beans

1 carrot, peeled and finely diced

1 stalk celery, finely diced

1 small onion, finely diced

2 cooking apples, peeled, cored, and finely diced

2 cups (473 ml) fresh apple cider

1/2 cup (118 ml) Marinated Lemon Purée

1 bay leaf

1/2 cup (60 g) pine nuts

1 teaspoon salt

1 teaspoon black pepper

Croutons or grilled French bread

Method

■ Soak the beans overnight in cold water.

■ To make the purée, first plunge the whole lemons into boiling water for 2 minutes. Drain, and cool. Then cut into thin slices, and remove the seeds.

■ In a small, lidded container, arrange a layer of lemon slices, and sprinkle it with some of the salt, sugar, garlic, and marjoram. Repeat this layering process until all the ingredients have been used. Pour the oil over the top, and cover tightly.

■ Place the container in the refrigerator for at least 2 days. (The layered ingredients will keep for up to 1 month if stored in this manner.) Then purée the contents in a blender.

■ Rinse the soaked beans, and drain them well. Place all the dip ingredients (except for the croutons, which will serve as a garnish) in a saucepan, and add enough cold water to cover. Bring to a simmer over medium heat, skimming and discarding any foam that rises to the top. Simmer for 1-1/2 hours, adding water if necessary to keep the beans covered.

■ When the beans are tender, remove them from the heat, and allow them to cool. Drain and save the liquid. Purée the beans in a blender or food processor, adding seasoning as desired; correct the thickness by adding more cider and/or the reserved bean-cooking liquid as necessary. The dip should be the consistency of thick applesauce; if it's too thick, it won't be spreadable.

■ Serve the bean purée on crispy croutons or grilled French bread.

INDIAN APPLE PUDDING

This traditional recipe dates back to the 1800s, and doesn't exactly reflect modern tastes. We tend to use more sugar than our forbears, and the unrefined flavor of molasses can seem foreign, but the blend of flavors is nevertheless fascinating. The dish can serve as a savory addition to a buffet meal, or, topped with a little light cream, as a dessert.

Yields
12 SERVINGS

HAVE ON HAND

Double boiler (optional)

3-quart (2.8 l) ovenproof casserole,
well greased

INGREDIENTS

6 cups (1.4 l) milk

1/2 vanilla bean

1/2 cup (60 g) fine yellow corn meal

2/3 cup (158 ml) molasses

2 tablespoons butter

1 teaspoon salt

1/2 teaspoon ginger

1/4 teaspoon nutmeg

1/8 teaspoon allspice

1/8 teaspoon cloves

1/4 teaspoon cinnamon

2-3/4 eating apples, peeled,
cored, and diced

1/4 eating apple, sliced

1/2 cup (118 ml) light cream,
flavored with 2 tablespoons Calvados
(apple brandy); optional

METHOD

■ Preheat the oven to 275°F (135°C). In a saucepan or in the top portion of a double boiler, scald 4 cups (946 g) of the milk over direct heat. Place the pan of scalded milk in a pan of boiling water (or fit the top of the double boiler into the bottom portion). Slowly add the corn meal to the milk, and cook for about 5 minutes, stirring continuously, until the mixture is thick.

■ Add the molasses, butter, salt, and spices. Mix well, and remove from the heat. Stir in the remaining 2 cups (473 ml) of cold milk, and mix in the diced apples. Pour the pudding into the prepared casserole, garnish the top with the reserved apple slices, and bake for 3 hours, or until the pudding is set and firm. Serve hot.

ROASTED MUSHROOM SOUP *with* CIDER STOCK

A model of simplicity, this flavorful soup becomes a complete meal when served with a hearty loaf of bread. Although other types of mushrooms can be used, the recipe calls for one of my favorite varieties—the yellow morel (Morchella esculenta). Because morels are often found in old apple orchards, I always associate the arrival of these delightful friends with the blossoming of apple trees. It's no wonder that the combination of cider stock and morels is sublime.

Yields
8 TO 10 SERVINGS OF SOUP

HAVE ON HAND

Hand-held blender

CIDER STOCK INGREDIENTS

4 cooking apples

6 medium carrots

6 leeks, roots and 1/2 of
green leaves removed

4 cups (280 g) Portabello (or other)
mushroom stems

3 tablespoons light cooking oil
(safflower or peanut)

2 tablespoons coriander seeds

1 gallon (3.8 l) fresh apple cider
or apple juice

2 tablespoons black peppercorns

12 sprigs fresh Italian parsley

12 sprigs fresh thyme

1 bay leaf

SOUP INGREDIENTS

2 cups (140 g) yellow morels

2 cups (140 g) oyster mushrooms

2 cups (140 g) button mushrooms

4 tablespoons clarified butter

1 teaspoon salt

1/2 teaspoon black pepper

3 tablespoons fresh marjoram leaves

1/4 cup (59 ml) Madeira

7 cups (1.7 l) Cider Stock
(see "Notes")

3 tablespoons heavy cream (optional)

METHOD

■ Preheat the oven to 300°F (149°C). Chop the unpeeled apples, unpeeled carrots, leeks, and mushroom stems into 2" (5.1 cm) cubes, discarding the hard, dried ends of the mushroom stems. Place these ingredients in a roasting pan, toss with the cooking oil, and add the whole coriander seeds. Roast until golden brown, about 2 hours, turning the ingredients 3 or 4 times during cooking.

■ Scrape the roasted vegetables into a stockpot. To loosen the browned bits sticking to the bottom of the roasting pan, pour in a cup of cold water, and scrape the loosened bits into the stockpot. (The process of retrieving these taste-laden bits is known as *deglazing*.)

■ Add the cider or apple juice, the remaining stock ingredients, and just enough cold water to cover them. Place the lid on the stockpot, leaving it slightly ajar, and heat the stock over medium-low heat. It should reach a simmer in about 1 hour. Simmer for 8 hours, adjusting the heat if necessary. Strain, cool, and refrigerate.

■ Wipe any dirt from the yellow morels and the oyster and button mushrooms, rinse well, and pat dry. Be sure to remove and discard the dried, hard parts of the stems.

■ Heat the clarified butter in a heavy skillet over medium heat. Add the whole mushrooms and sauté, tossing once or twice during the first few minutes. The mushrooms will begin to render their liquid. After 5 minutes, reduce the heat to medium-low. At this time, pour 7 cups (1.7 l) of the stock back into the stockpot, and bring to a simmer.

■ Continue to cook the mushrooms, browning them and allowing them to render all their liquid. You may need to add some additional butter to keep them from sticking to the pan or burning. Stir once every 3 minutes while they cook. Once the liquid has evaporated, add the salt, pepper, 2 tablespoons of the marjoram leaves, and the Madeira, and allow the wine to evaporate completely. Then add all but 6 tablespoons of the browned mushrooms to the simmering stock. Turn the heat up to bring the stock to a slow boil, and cook for 15 minutes. Check the seasonings, and correct if necessary.

■ Purée the finished soup with a hand-held blender. (You may use a jar blender instead, but be careful when you turn it on, as these devices tend to spill out their contents!)

■ Divide the soup among 6 heated soup bowls, garnish with the remaining marjoram leaves and mushrooms, and, if desired, drip a little heavy cream into each bowl. Serve immediately.

Notes: The Cider Stock ingredients and cooking instructions will yield about 1-1/2 gallons (5.7 l) of finished stock—more than you'll need to make this soup. Plan on freezing the rest for other uses.

You'll need to make the stock at least 24 hours in advance of preparing the soup. For extra stock-making tips, refer to the recipe on page 134.

A P P L E F R I T T E R S *and* C A L V A D O S C R E A M

Offer this as a dessert—it's especially wonderful when served with a shot of very cold Calvados (apple brandy)—or as a delectable breakfast dish. The cream sauce is a warm custard, delicately flavored with Calvados. Do keep in mind that the batter must be prepared 3 to 12 hours before serving.

Yields
6 SERVINGS

*Electric deep fryer
or 1-1/2-quart (1.4 l) saucepan*

Deep-frying thermometer

FRITTER INGREDIENTS

1-1/4 cups (156 g) all-purpose flour

*1 cup plus 2 tablespoons (266 ml)
apple juice or white wine*

1/2 teaspoon lemon zest

1/4 teaspoon salt

1 egg white

3 eating apples

Oil for deep-frying

CALVADOS CREAM AND GARNISH INGREDIENTS

1 cup (237 ml) half-and-half

1/2 cup (118 ml) heavy cream

1/2 vanilla bean, split

4 egg yolks

1/2 cup (100 g) granulated sugar

3 tablespoons Calvados

1/8 teaspoon nutmeg

1 tablespoon confectioner's sugar

Slivers of unpeeled green apple

■ Prepare the batter by mixing together the flour, apple juice or wine, lemon zest, and salt. Whisk until smooth, and refrigerate for 3 to 12 hours.

■ Before preparing the fritters, set the deep fryer at 375°F (190°C). Whip the egg white until soft peaks are formed, and fold it into the batter. (If you fry the fritters too far in advance, they'll get soggy.)

■ Peel the apples, cut them into thin slices, and pat dry with a towel. Dip each slice into the batter, letting any excess batter drip off. Fry the slices, a few at a time, for about 2 minutes or until golden. Drain on paper towels or brown paper, and keep warm until served.

■ Next, make the Calvados cream. Combine the half-and-half, heavy cream, and vanilla bean in a saucepan. Heat to scald, but do not boil.

■ In a mixing bowl, beat together the egg yolks and sugar until the graininess of the sugar disappears (about 3 minutes). When the cream mixture is hot, but not boiling, carefully and very slowly pour half of it into the yolk-and-sugar mixture, stirring continuously as you do. Heating the yolks gradually in this fashion (a process known as *tempering*) helps prevent them from curdling.

■ Lower the heat under the remaining cream mixture to medium-low. Gradually add the yolk-and-cream mixture to the cream mixture, stirring continuously. (This recipe can be made in a double boiler, but I prefer to live dangerously. As long as you keep stirring and don't let the heat get too high, you'll be fine!)

■ Cook the custard until it's thick enough to coat the stirring spoon without dripping from it. If you notice little granules forming, it's definitely time to stop, as the egg protein is beginning to curdle. Remove from the heat when thick. Add the Calvados, stir in the nutmeg, and remove the vanilla bean.

■ Divide the custard equally among 6 plates, and place the warm fritters on top. Dust with confectioner's sugar, garnish with apple slivers, and serve.

APPLE CHARLOTTE

It's difficult to describe this old-world dessert accurately. Is it a bread pudding? No. Is it a cake? Maybe. Is it wonderful? I haven't come across anything quite as delicious in my culinary career.

Yields
6 TO 8 SERVINGS

4-cup (946 ml) charlotte mold

Pan at least two-thirds as deep as mold

Bamboo skewer or broom straw

INGREDIENTS

2 cups (250 g) all-purpose flour

2 teaspoons baking powder

1 cup (200 g) granulated sugar

2 eggs

6 tablespoons butter, melted

1 teaspoon vanilla

1 cup (237 ml) water

1 cup (200 g) granulated sugar

6 large tart apples, peeled, cored,
and thinly sliced

1 eating apple, sliced, for garnish

1 cup (237 ml) heavy cream,
lightly whipped with
1 tablespoon granulated sugar

■ Preheat the oven to 375°F (190°C). To make the "cake," first combine the flour, baking powder, and 1 cup (200 g) of sugar. Beat the eggs lightly, and mix them into the dry ingredients. Add the melted butter and the vanilla, and stir well.

■ Combine the water and the second cup (200 g) of sugar in a heavy saucepan over high heat. Make sure that any sugar grains sticking to the sides are washed down, as they will cause the sugar to recrystallize. Boil the mixture until the water has evaporated and the sugar begins to change from white to light tan in color; swirl the pan gently as the sugar cooks. Do be careful! The pan is very hot at this stage; if you splatter the sugar, it will stick and burn. Continue cooking and swirling until the sugar is a deep auburn color.

■ Working quickly, pour the caramelized sugar into the charlotte mold, coating the inside completely, and arrange a layer of tart apple slices in a decorative pattern on the bottom of the mold. (This apple layer will be the top of the charlotte.) Then build the charlotte by alternating thin layers of cake batter with layers of tart apple slices, finishing the mold with an apple layer.

■ Place the mold in a pan that's at least two-thirds as deep as the mold. Pour hot water into the pan, halfway up the mold, and bake for 1 hour. To test, insert a bamboo skewer or broom straw; it should come out clean. If the cake adheres to the skewer, continue baking, checking every 5 minutes or so.

■ Allow the finished charlotte to cool for about 30 minutes, and then unmold. Garnish with fresh apple slices or a curled apple peel, and serve warm with lightly whipped and sweetened cream.

Note: To clean hardened caramel from the pan in which you've cooked it, fill the pan with hot water, and bring the water to a boil.

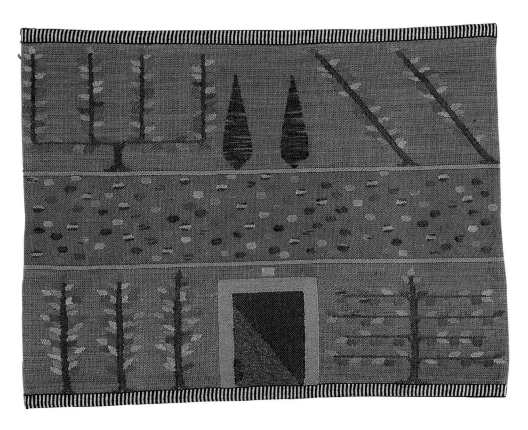

ESPALIERS AND CORDONS
(BROCADED WEAVING)
LAURA FOSTER NICHOLSON

CHOCOLATE TRUFFLES *with* CIDER CALVADOS GANACHE

Making chocolates is one of my passions—second only to cooking with apples—so this recipe, which combines cider and chocolate, is one of my favorites. Don't be intimidated by the mention of "tempering" chocolate; this is simply the process of cooling the chocolate and mixing it completely before using it.

Yields
40 WALNUT-SIZED TRUFFLES

Double boiler

3/4-ounce (22 ml) ice-cream scoop

Silicone baking paper

Candy thermometer

INGREDIENTS

1-1/2 pounds (680 g)
high-quality semisweet chocolate

1 cup (237 ml) heavy cream

2 tablespoons Calvados (apple brandy)

3 tablespoons fresh apple cider

3 ounces (85 g) white chocolate (optional)

Notes: The ganache, which is a combination of heavy cream and chocolate, must be made 24 hours in advance; it needs time to set up before handling.

The completed truffles shouldn't be refrigerated, as they'll be ruined by the moisture that collects on them. Store at room temperature instead; the truffles will keep for at least a week.

■ To make the ganache, first chop 1 pound (454 g) of the chocolate into small pieces, and combine with the cream, Calvados, and cider in a double boiler over simmering water. Stir until completely melted. If the chocolate starts to separate, remove the pan from the heat, and continue stirring until the mixture cools and comes back together. Be careful not to overheat.

■ Pour the ganache into a container just large enough to hold it, and allow it to cure for 24 hours at a temperature no higher than 68°F (20°C).

■ After the ganache has cured, spread some silicon baking paper on your work surface. Using the ice-cream scoop, arrange walnut-sized portions of ganache on the paper. Refrigerate the ganache portions (just move the whole sheet of paper) for 5 minutes. Then roll each scoop into a round shape. (If the chocolate is too soft to handle, let it sit a bit longer in the refrigerator.) Place the rounded pieces onto a clean sheet of baking paper, and let them rest for 30 minutes.

■ While the ganache is resting, set aside 1 ounce (28 g) of the remaining chocolate. To melt and temper the rest, first place it in a double boiler over simmering water, stirring continuously until the chocolate is smooth. Remove the melted chocolate from the heat, and stir in the remaining 1-ounce (28 g) portion. Let the chocolate sit for about 5 minutes.

■ At this stage, professional chocolatiers spread the chocolate on a marble slab to speed up the cooling process, but stirring it works just as well. Stir to cool, testing the temperature periodically by touching a bit of chocolate to your lower lip. When completely melted, it will be very warm—100°F to 120°F (38°C to 49°C). When the chocolate has reached the proper working temperature (82°F to 86°F or 28°C to 30°C), it will feel cool on your lip and will have started to thicken.

■ Now you're ready to make the truffles by coating the ganache rounds with chocolate. Organize your ingredients and utensils first. If you're right-handed, place the sheet of ganache rounds on your left; the melted, cooled chocolate in front of you; and a silicone-paper lined baking sheet on your right. Dip your hands into the chocolate to coat them. Pick up a ganache round with your left hand, roll it between both hands to coat it with chocolate, and place the truffle on the clean paper with your right hand. Recoat your hands, and repeat until all the rounds have been coated. Allow the chocolate to harden at room temperature.

■ To create the white chocolate "filigree" on your truffles, first melt and temper some white chocolate. Dip the tips of your fingers into it, shake most of the chocolate back into the bowl, and then briskly fling your hand back and forth over the truffles to disperse thin threads of chocolate over them.

CIDER LEMON SORBET *with* APPLE CRISP

You don't need an ice-cream or sorbet freezer for this recipe. In fact, I prefer the method that follows because it produces a sorbet with a creamier texture. The simple syrup recipe that serves as the base for this dessert—a boiled sugar-water that is frequently used in dessert making—will serve many of your cooking needs and can be refrigerated for up to 3 months.

Yields
6 SERVINGS

Shallow baking dish or pan

6 four-ounce (118 ml) round porcelain baking molds, 3" (7.6 cm) in diameter and 1-1/2" (3.8 cm) deep

SIMPLE SYRUP INGREDIENTS

(see "Notes")

2 cups (473 ml) water

2-5/8 cups (525 g) granulated sugar

6 whole coriander seeds

1 cinnamon stick

SORBET INGREDIENTS

(see "Notes")

3 cups (710 ml) fresh apple cider

1-1/2 cups (355 ml) Simple Syrup

Juice of 1 lemon

2 egg whites

TOPPING INGREDIENTS

3/4 cup (90 g) all-purpose flour

1 tablespoon granulated sugar

2/3 cup (147 g) light brown sugar

6 tablespoons unsalted butter, softened

2/3 cup (80 g) chopped pecans

APPLE CRISP AND GARNISH INGREDIENTS

5 medium cooking apples

3 tablespoons unsalted butter

5 tablespoons light brown sugar

1/4 teaspoon nutmeg

1/4 teaspoon ginger

1/4 teaspoon allspice

1/4 teaspoon coriander

1 tablespoon cinnamon

1/2 teaspoon salt

1 teaspoon vanilla extract

1 tablespoon all-purpose flour

Fresh mint leaves

■ Place the sugar in the saucepan. Add the water, making sure to wash any grains of sugar down and off the sides of the pan. (Sugar that remains undissolved can cause the syrup to become grainy after cooking. If this should happen, add an additional 1/4 cup or 59 ml of water, and bring back to a boil.) Place the pan over medium-high heat. Add the coriander seeds and cinnamon stick, and boil for 1 minute.

■ Remove from the heat, and allow to cool. Store in the refrigerator until ready to use.

■ To make the sorbet, mix together the cider, simple syrup, and lemon juice. Pour the mixture into a shallow baking dish or pan that is large enough to hold it in a layer 1" (2.5 cm) deep. Place the pan in the freezer, making sure that it's level. Once every 30 minutes, stir the sorbet with a fork. As the mixture begins to freeze, stir it more frequently, mixing the colder edges in toward the warmer center. When the entire mixture is quite slushy, whip the egg whites to soft peaks, and fold them in. Allow the sorbet to sit in the freezer for at least 30 minutes before serving.

■ To make the topping, first mix together the flour and granulated sugar. Then add the brown sugar, soft butter, and chopped pecans, and mix well.

■ Preheat the oven to 425°F (218°C). To prepare the apple crisp, combine all the ingredients except for the flour and mint leaves in a saucepan. Simmer over medium heat for 3 minutes. Add the flour, mix well, and cook for 2 more minutes. Fill the baking molds with the mixture, and cover each one with pecan topping. Place the molds on a baking sheet, and bake for 30 minutes. Allow to cool for 5 minutes before serving. (If you'd like to prepare the crisps in advance, fill the molds as directed, wrap them tightly with plastic food wrap, and refrigerate for up to 3 days before baking.)

■ When the crisps are done, scoop each one onto a serving dish. Spoon out a portion of the sorbet onto each dish, and garnish with fresh mint leaves.

Notes: Allow at least 1 hour to cook and cool the simple syrup, or make it well in advance and refrigerate until ready to use.

Allow at least 4 to 5 hours for the sorbet to freeze, but don't let it sit for more than a day, as it's somewhat delicate in texture. The longer the sorbet is in the freezer, the harder it becomes.

APPLE PRALINES

This recipe, which is a very old one indeed, takes us back in time. The candy is a refined version of a children's favorite—caramel apples. Don't use tart cooking apples, as the cooking will turn them into sauce.

Yields
6 SERVINGS

INGREDIENTS

Juice of 3 lemons

*6 small dessert apples, peeled, cored,
and thinly sliced*

1 cup (200 g) granulated sugar

1/4 cup (59 ml) water

Caramels (optional)

METHOD

■ Place the lemon juice in the saucepan, and bring to a boil over high heat. Toss the sliced apples in the juice, and cook for 2 minutes. Remove the pan from the heat, and let the apples cool; they'll absorb the lemon juice as they do.

■ Mix the sugar and water. Bring to a boil over medium heat, and cook until most of the water evaporates and the sugar looks syrupy. Continue to cook the sugar until it becomes a light golden color.

■ Carefully drop in the apple slices, and cook them in the caramelized sugar for 3 minutes, tossing twice with the tip of a fork. Remove the apples from the syrup, and drain them on a wire rack until cool.

■ The pralines may be served by themselves or with caramels. They can also be used as a garnish for other desserts.

Note: These pralines do not keep well, so make them no more than a day in advance. Store at room temperature in a sealed plastic container.

THE *Lady Apple*

The Lady apple, a particularly flavorful apple variety that is sometimes difficult to find, probably originated in France during medieval times, although some researchers believe that it may be a descendant of an ancient Roman variety.

Also known as the Pommes d'Api, the Lady apple is one of the oldest recorded varieties of apple in existence. It was grown in the gardens of Louis XIII at Orleans and was one of only seven varieties deemed suitable for his table.

This small, somewhat flattened, and long-lasting apple is creamy yellow to deep crimson in color, depending on its exposure to the sun. Try to avoid peeling Lady apples, as their skins have a wonderful flavor. Lady apples may be eaten fresh or cooked, or used to make cider.

Particularly valued during Colonial times, when it was in high demand around Christmas, the Lady apple has for centuries adorned tables as a decorative feature and is still commonly used in wreaths, garlands, and centerpieces.

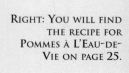

RIGHT: YOU WILL FIND THE RECIPE FOR POMMES À L'EAU-DE-VIE ON PAGE 25.

Apple Tart *with* Lemon Cream

The most memorable dishes are those that combine simplicity, elegance, and excellent ingredients. Crisp, flaky puff pastry, tart lemon cream, and fresh apples combine to make this recipe a wonderful finish to any meal. I have not provided a puff pastry recipe here, as excellent pastry can be purchased at specialty food shops.

Yields
6 SERVINGS

3 eating apples, peeled and thinly sliced

Juice of 1 lemon

1/2 pound (227 g) puff pastry

12 tablespoons unsalted butter

3/4 cup (150 g) granulated sugar

LEMON CREAM AND GARNISH INGREDIENTS

1 cup (237 ml) milk

1/2 cup (118 ml) heavy cream

1/2 vanilla bean

6 egg yolks

2/3 cup (130 g) granulated sugar

1 teaspoon lemon zest

Juice of 1/2 lemon

1 tablespoon orange liqueur

2 tablespoons granulated sugar

Lemon peel curls

■ Sprinkle the apple slices with the lemon juice. Preheat the oven to 400°F (205°C).

■ Roll out the puff pastry to 1/4" (6 mm) or less in thickness—the thinner the better. Cut the pastry into 6 circles, each at least 8" (20.3 cm) in diameter or almost as large as the dishes you plan to use for service.

■ With the point of a sharp knife, score a circle 1/2" (1.3 cm) in from the outer edge of each pastry. The apples will extend only to this scored mark, which will help to form an edge when the pastry bakes. Arrange the apples within the scored circles. Dot each pastry with 1 tablespoon of butter, and sprinkle each one with 1 tablespoon of sugar. Bake for 15 minutes, remove from the oven, and dot with the rest of the butter and sugar. Bake the pastries for 10 more minutes.

■ As the tarts bake, prepare the lemon cream. Heat the combined milk, heavy cream, and vanilla bean, but don't bring the liquid to a boil. In a saucepan (not over heat), whisk the egg yolks, adding the sugar a spoonful at a time and whisking it in rapidly until the mixture is pale yellow and all the sugar has dissolved.

■ Remove the vanilla bean from the hot milk, and then pour the milk into the egg mixture in a slow, steady stream, stirring it constantly with a rubber spatula. Set the mixture over medium-low heat, continuing to stir it constantly and making sure to reach all the edges. As with all custards, this one should be cooked slowly and should not be overcooked. The custard is done when it will hold an edge as you draw your finger across the custard-coated spatula. If small grains appear in the custard, remove the saucepan from the heat immediately, plunge its bottom into cold water, and stir vigorously to stop the cooking.

■ Mix the zest, lemon juice, and orange liqueur together, and then stir them into the custard sauce. Keep the sauce warm.

■ When the tarts are done, sprinkle a little more sugar on top, and place them under the broiler to caramelize the sugar. (Believe it or not, restaurants often use propane torches to do this!) Place a tart on each serving dish, spoon a little lemon cream over the top, and garnish with small curls of lemon peel. Pass the remaining cream separately.

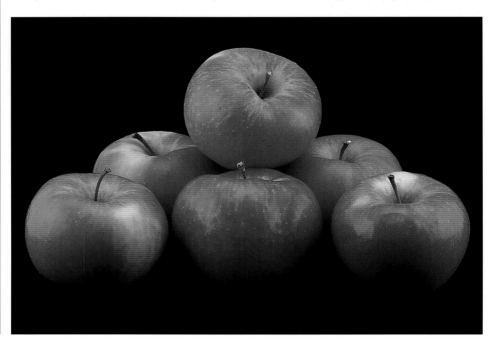

CALVADOS *and* CIDER SOUFFLÉ

Soufflés don't have to be intimidating, but it helps to think of them as first dates: Don't keep them waiting! Plan to serve them at the beginning of the meal or at the end, when you'll have the most control over their timing. This soufflé, of course, should be served as a dessert.

Yields
6 SERVINGS

HAVE ON HAND

6 six-ounce (178 ml) soufflé cups

SOUFFLÉ INGREDIENTS

2 tablespoons butter

7 tablespoons granulated sugar

1-1/4 (296 ml) cups milk

3 tablespoons all-purpose flour

1/8 teaspoon ginger

1/8 teaspoon cloves

1/8 teaspoon nutmeg

2 tablespoons Apple Cider Reduction

2 tablespoons Calvados (apple brandy)

6 egg yolks

12 egg whites

1 eating apple

CALVADOS-FLAVORED WHIPPED CREAM INGREDIENTS

1/2 cup (118 ml) heavy whipping cream

1 tablespoon confectioner's sugar

2 tablespoons Calvados (apple brandy)

METHOD

■ Preheat the oven to 425°F (218°C). Coat the soufflé cups with the butter and 3 tablespoons of the sugar.

■ Combine the milk and remaining sugar in a cold saucepan, stirring well to dissolve the sugar. Stir in the flour thoroughly, and then add the spices and apple cider reduction. Cook this mixture over medium heat, stirring constantly, until the sauce has thickened. Taste periodically, and remove from the heat when the raw flour flavor disappears. Stir in the Calvados and 6 unbeaten egg yolks, and cool to lukewarm.

■ Whip the egg whites to firm peaks. (Do not overwhip, or the whites will become grainy, and the soufflé will break apart when cooked.) Fold 1/4 of the egg whites into the milk-and-yolk mixture. Then, using a rubber spatula, carefully fold this mixture back into the remaining egg whites, folding over only 3 or 4 times.

■ Divide the mixture among the soufflé dishes. Run a spatula once around the inner edge of each soufflé dish to help the soufflé rise straight up.

■ Peel, core, and cut the eating apple into thin slices. Carefully slide 2 or 3 slices into the middle of each soufflé. Bake for 10 minutes or until the soufflés have risen and are golden brown.

■ While the soufflés are baking, make the whipped cream. Combine the heavy cream and confectioner's sugar in a medium-sized bowl. With a wire whisk, steadily beat the cream until it forms soft peaks. Add the Calvados and continue beating until the cream stiffens a little more.

■ Serve the soufflés as soon as they're done, offering the whipped cream on the side.

To make wonderful sorbet, you'll want to add two things to the listed ingredients: patience and a good sense of timing. Don't worry—both qualities can be learned!

Yields
6 SERVINGS

ADDITIONAL AND BASIC
RECIPES INCLUDED

Apple-Flavored Simple Syrup from
Pommes à l'Eau-de-Vie
(PAGES 24–25)

Apple Cider Reduction
(OPTIONAL; PAGE 132)

Mixer fitted with paddle blade

Baking or silicone paper

9" x 12" (22.9 x 30.5 cm) dish or pan

6 teacups

COOKIE INGREDIENTS

3-1/2 tablespoons butter, softened

1/2 cup (100 g) sugar

2 egg whites

5 tablespoons cake flour

1/3 cup (40 g) raw, ground almonds

Zest of 1 lemon

1 teaspoon lemon juice

Butter for baking paper

SORBET AND OPTIONAL SAUCE INGREDIENTS

(see "Notes")

2 cups (473 ml) fresh apple cider

1 cup (237 ml) Apple-Flavored Simple Syrup

Juice of 1 lemon

2 egg whites

Apple Cider Reduction (optional)

Fresh raspberries (optional)

■ Preheat the oven to 425°F (218°C).

■ In a mixer fitted with a paddle blade, cream the butter and sugar for about 5 minutes or until the mixture is fluffy and all the sugar has dissolved. Turn the mixer speed to low, add the unbeaten egg whites, and beat for a few more seconds.

■ Scrape the sides of the bowl to combine all the ingredients. Sift the flour, and fold it into the butter mixture on low speed. Add the almonds, zest, and lemon juice. Fold together on low speed for 10 seconds.

■ Cover a baking sheet with buttered baking paper. Using a tablespoon, drop the dough onto the sheet in 6 equal amounts, leaving plenty of space between portions. Using the back of the spoon, spread out the dough into very thin circles. Bake for 8 minutes, until the edges of the cookies are dark and their centers are light brown.

■ With a metal spatula, quickly remove the cookies, drape them over 6 inverted tea cups, and press them over the cups to form bowl shapes. If the dough becomes too cool to be shaped, place the pan back in the oven for a few seconds to reheat. Store the cooled cookies in an airtight container until ready to use.

■ To make the sorbet, first combine the cider, apple-flavored simple syrup, and lemon juice. Pour into a pan or shallow dish, and place the pan in the freezer, making sure that the pan is level. Check in 1 hour. As the mixture begins to freeze around the edges, stir it with a fork to distribute the ice crystals evenly. Check again in another hour or so, and stir again. When the sorbet is completely slushy, whip the egg whites to soft peaks, and, using a wire whisk, fold them into the slushy mixture. Allow the sorbet to freeze for another hour.

■ To serve the sorbet, spoon it into the lemon-cookie cups. A little apple cider reduction, served on the side, makes a wonderful sauce, and fresh raspberries make a colorful garnish.

Notes: Leave yourself at least four hours to prepare the sorbet. If you like, you can make it a day or two in advance.

The pan in which you make the sorbet should hold it in a 1/2"-thick (1.3 cm) layer.

You don't need an ice-cream freezer, but you can certainly use one if you like. Just add the egg whites about two-thirds of the way through the cycle.

APPLE BREAD PUDDING *with* CINNAMON APPLE ICE CREAM

Some dishes, because they're so simple, so delicious, and so satisfying, have caught the fancy of generations; their popularity never fades. Bread pudding is one of those dishes. Serve it with the ice cream described here, and you'll make lifelong friends in the process.

Yields

6 SERVINGS PUDDING AND 1 QUART (.9 L) ICE CREAM

Apple Cider Reduction
(PAGE 132)

HAVE ON HAND

Metal mixing bowl or double boiler

2-quart (1.9 l) ice-cream freezer

6-cup (1.4 l) baking dish

Roasting pan larger than the baking dish

ICE CREAM INGREDIENTS

(see "Notes")

5 egg yolks

1/2 cup (100 g) granulated sugar

1 quart (.9 l) half-and-half

1 teaspoon cinnamon

1/8 teaspoon nutmeg

1/8 teaspoon coriander

1/4 cup (59 ml) heavy cream

2 tablespoons Apple Cider Reduction

PUDDING INGREDIENTS

7 tablespoons butter, softened

8 slices firm, white bread

6 eggs

1/4 cup (50 g) granulated sugar

1/2 teaspoon cinnamon

1 cup (237 ml) heavy cream

3/4 cup (177 ml) Apple Cider Reduction

1/2 cup (152 g) quince or apple jelly

*4 cooking apples, peeled,
cored, and sliced*

2 tablespoons confectioner's sugar

■ To prepare the ice cream, begin by combining the yolks and sugar in a metal mixing bowl. Beat well with a wire whisk until the sugar has dissolved. Fill a saucepan halfway with water, and bring the water to a boil. Place the metal mixing bowl over the water, and cook for 3 to 4 minutes or until the yolks thicken. Set aside.

■ In a separate saucepan, combine the half-and-half and the spices. Scald this mixture over medium heat by bringing it to a temperature just below boiling point.

■ Slowly combine the hot liquid with the egg-and-sugar mixture. Then place the metal bowl back over the hot water, and cook for about 1 minute, stirring continuously with a rubber spatula, until the mixture thickens. To test for thickness, lift the spatula from the mixture, and run your finger along its surface. If the mixture is runny and fills the streak, continue cooking. (If you see grains forming, the egg yolks are beginning to curdle from overcooking. Remove the pan from the heat immediately, and plunge it into cold water while stirring vigorously to cool the custard.)

■ When the mixture has thickened, remove the bowl from the heat. Add the heavy cream and the apple cider reduction. Mix well, and allow the custard to cool completely before proceeding.

■ Place the cooled custard in your ice-cream freezer, and follow the manufacturer's instructions for freezing. Place the finished ice cream in a container with a lid, set it in your freezer, and allow it to "cure" for 1 hour before serving.

■ Begin the pudding as the ice cream cures. Preheat the oven to 325°F (163°C).

■ Spread 2 tablespoons of the butter over one side of the bread slices. Then cut each slice into quarters. Coat the baking dish with 2 more tablespoons of butter, and layer the bread pieces inside.

■ Whisk together the eggs, sugar, and cinnamon until well blended. Set aside. In a saucepan over medium heat, combine the cream, apple cider reduction, and jelly, and bring to a simmer. Then whisk together the egg and cream mixtures, and pour over the bread.

■ Place the baking dish in a roasting pan, and pour in enough hot water to reach halfway up the sides of the dish. Bake for 45 to 50 minutes, until the custard has set. While the pudding is baking, sauté the apple slices in the remaining butter until golden, and set aside.

■ Remove the custard from the oven, dust with confectioner's sugar, and place under a preheated broiler until the sugar is caramelized. Top with the browned apples, and serve with the ice cream.

Notes: The ice cream must be made at least 6 hours before serving. If you like, you can prepare the cooked custard with which the ice cream is made up to 24 hours in advance; just cover it tightly and refrigerate.

If you don't have an ice-cream freezer, substitute store-bought ice cream or one of the sorbet recipes in this book (see pages 112–113 and 120–121).

APPLE MOLASSES COOKIES

Don't let the description "cookies" deceive you. These sandwiches are hearty enough—and rich enough—for any die-hard dessert fan. They make a great addition to picnics and a superb grand finale to a casual outdoor party. Be sure to hide a few for yourself; if you turn your back, they'll disappear.

Yields
12 COOKIE SANDWICHES

Walnut Apple Butter
(PAGE 27)

HAVE ON HAND

Mixer fitted with paddle blade

Baking or silicone paper

INGREDIENTS

(see "Note")

1 cup (237 ml) Walnut Apple Butter

1-1/2 teaspoons ginger

1/2 teaspoon nutmeg

1 teaspoon baking powder

1 cup (230 g) butter

1 cup (220 g) light brown sugar

2 eggs

1/2 cup (118 ml) molasses

1/4 cup (59 ml) fresh apple cider

3 cups (375 g) all-purpose flour

1/2 cup (60 g) confectioner's sugar

1 tablespoon cinnamon

1/2 teaspoon ginger

METHOD

■ Make the walnut apple butter first, and set it aside.

■ Mix together the ginger, nutmeg, and baking powder in a large mixing bowl. Blend together the molasses and apple cider in a separate mixing bowl.

■ Cream the butter and brown sugar together in a mixer fitted with a paddle blade for 4 minutes at medium-high speed. Reduce the speed, and add the eggs. With the mixer still set at low, add the molasses mixture and spices to the butter and sugar. Then add the flour, and blend well.

■ Shape the dough into a 3"-diameter (7.6 cm) log, wrap it in plastic film, and refrigerate for at least 1 hour, until the dough is firm.

■ Preheat the oven to 425°F (218°C). Line the baking pans with baking paper. Remove the plastic food wrap from the cookie dough, slice the log into twenty-four 1/2"-thick (1.3 cm) cookies, and arrange the slices on the baking paper. Bake for 10 minutes until golden brown, and cool on a wire rack.

■ If you've refrigerated the walnut apple butter, bring it to room temperature before spreading it to make the cookie sandwiches. Combine the confectioner's sugar, cinnamon, and ginger, and dust the completed cookies with this spicy mixture before serving.

Note: The cookies will require at least 2 hours to prepare, so leave plenty of time before you load the picnic basket.

APPLE GRATIN *and* CIDER BUTTER
with PISTACHIO ICE CREAM

This is a dish to serve to a cantankerous mother-in-law. Although the cider butter takes quite a bit of time to prepare, the finished dish is so rich and creamy and its flavors are so well set off by pistachio ice cream, that you'll leave her thinking you're quite the bargain.

Yields
6 SERVINGS

Mixer fitted with paddle blade

Heatproof serving dishes

APPLE GRATIN INGREDIENTS

4 cups (946 ml) water

*1 cup plus 2 tablespoons (225 g)
granulated sugar*

1 vanilla bean, split

Juice of 1 lemon

*6 medium-tart cooking apples,
peeled, cored, and sliced*

FRANGIPANE CREAM
INGREDIENTS

1/2 cup (115 g) butter, softened

*1 cup plus 2 tablespoons (225 g)
granulated sugar*

2 eggs

*4 ounces (113 g) raw almonds,
ground into meal*

CIDER BUTTER INGREDIENTS

*2 cooking apples, peeled, cored,
and sliced*

1 cup (230 g) butter

1 cup (237 ml) fresh apple cider

Note: Don't forget to stock up on pistachio ice cream; instructions for making it aren't provided here. You'll need 1 quart (.9 l) for 6 servings.

■ To make the apple gratin, first bring the water, sugar, vanilla bean, and lemon juice to a boil. Add the apples, reduce to a simmer, and cook until the apples are tender— about 5 minutes. Drain, discarding the vanilla bean and reserving the cooking liquid for making simple syrups (see pages 113 and 121) or for cooking another batch of apples. Set the apples aside.

■ Next comes the frangipane cream. In a mixer fitted with a paddle blade, cream the butter and sugar together at medium speed for 4 minutes, until the sugar is well blended. Add the eggs, and continue beating until the mixture turns white and fluffy. Stir in the ground almonds, and set aside.

■ To start the cider butter, sauté the cooking apples in 8 tablespoons (115 g) of the butter over medium heat for about 5 minutes, or until golden. Add the apple cider to the pan, and reduce by one-third. Remove from the heat, allow to cool, and then purée. Beat in the remaining butter.

■ Preheat the broiler. Arrange the cooked apple slices in circles on individual heatproof dishes. Place a scoop of the frangipane cream in the center of each dish, and place the dish under the broiler, until the cream is golden brown. Top with a dollop of cider butter, and serve with pistachio ice cream.

Pumpkin and Apple Tart with Currants

Pumpkins, like beets, appeal to some folks but not to others. I find it hard to resist their creamy texture and slightly exotic flavor—especially in this dish.

Yields
8 TO 12 SERVINGS

Two 8" (20.3 cm) tart pans

PASTRY INGREDIENTS
(FOR 2 TART SHELLS)

(see "Notes")

1-1/2 cups (188 g) all-purpose flour

1/2 cup (62 g) bread flour

1/2 teaspoon salt

1 tablespoon granulated sugar

1 teaspoon baking powder

10 tablespoons butter, softened but cool

*4 tablespoons heavy cream
beaten with 1 egg yolk*

FILLING INGREDIENTS
(FOR 1 TART SHELL)

*1-1/2 cups (366 g) cooked pumpkin
(see "Notes")*

*3 medium cooking apples, peeled, cored,
and diced*

*1/2 cup (118 ml) sweet white dessert wine
(sauterne, for example)*

2 tablespoons honey

1/2 cup (70 g) granulated sugar

4 eggs, slightly beaten

1/2 cup (56 g) currants

1 teaspoon cinnamon

1/2 teaspoon chopped, fresh thyme

1/8 teaspoon grated nutmeg

1/4 teaspoon chopped, fresh rosemary

1/4 teaspoon chopped, fresh marjoram

1/4 teaspoon salt

1 eating apple, sliced

■ Place all the dry ingredients in a mixing bowl, and stir them together. Cut in the butter with a pastry cutter or 2 forks, until the mixture is the texture of oatmeal. Work in the liquid ingredients, and form the dough into a ball. (You may also mix the dough in a food processor or in a mixer fitted with a flat blade.) If any unblended bits of flour remain, add a few drops of cream to bind them together. The dough should be moist, but not sticky.

■ Divide the dough in half, and freeze one-half for later use. Then, either roll out the remaining half immediately, or refrigerate it for 1/2 hour first to make it firmer. Fit the rolled dough into an 8" (20.3 cm) tart pan, and place the pan in the freezer while you assemble the filling.

■ Preheat the oven to 450°F (232°C). In a mixing bowl, combine all the filling ingredients, and mix well. Place the filling into the prepared pastry shell, top with apple slices, and bake for 15 minutes. Then turn down the heat to 350°F (177°C), and bake for another 40 minutes. Allow to cool before serving.

Notes: This recipe yields enough pastry for two tart shells; freeze one-half of the dough for future use, or double the filling recipe to make 2 tarts.

Canned pumpkin will do for this recipe, but you may want to cook your own. Cut a fresh pumpkin into slices, and remove the seeds and stringy interior. Place the slices on a baking sheet or in a roasting pan, and roast in a preheated 350°F (177°C) oven for about 1 hour or until the pumpkin is very tender. Remove from the oven, allow to cool, and, using a heavy spoon, scrape the cooked pumpkin from the skin, placing it in a bowl. Using a fork, mash until no lumps remain.

APPLE LEATHER

In high school, I had a friend whose family was from Lebanon, and on the bus to school, we often shared food. One favorite from my friend was a chewy apricot "leather." Many years later, I was delighted to discover that leathers have traditionally been made from apples, too. Apple leather is a great snack for children because it satisfies their craving for sweets, but adults will also find its concentrated flavor and mellow sweetness completely intoxicating.

Yields
TWO 11 x 16 (27.9 x 40.6 CM) SHEETS OF LEATHER

Two 11" x 16" (27.9 x 40.6 cm) baking sheets with sides, well greased

Waxed paper

INGREDIENTS

(see "Note")

12 medium apples, peeled, cored, and diced

1 cup (237 ml) fresh apple cider

1/4 teaspoon cinnamon

1/8 teaspoon nutmeg

1/4 teaspoon coriander

Juice of 1/2 lemon

Cornstarch

METHOD

■ Combine all the ingredients except the cornstarch in a saucepan, and cook over low heat, stirring frequently, until the apples are the consistency of runny jam. This may take up to 1 hour.

■ Divide the apple mixture between the two prepared baking sheets, spreading the sauce in an even layer, about 1/4" (6 mm) thick.

■ Set the pans in a warm oven, on its lowest setting, with the door slightly ajar, and leave in place for about 6 hours.

■ Remove the leather from the oven, and protect it by draping a tea towel over the top of each pan. Place the covered pans in an out-of-the-way place overnight.

■ The next day, return the uncovered pans to the warm oven for another 6 hours. Remove, cover again, and allow the leather to air-dry for up to 1 week. (Drying times will vary depending on humidity levels.)

■ To store the leather once it has dried thoroughly, dust it lightly with a little cornstarch, place each sheet on a sheet of waxed paper, and roll up the paper and leather into logs. To eat, simply unwrap, tear off a piece, and enjoy.

Note. Feel free to use any combination of your favorite apple spices in place of those suggested.

BASIC RECIPES

The recipes in this section—from the tangy cider reduction to the traditional applesauce—serve as foundations for a number of other recipes in this book. They're all relatively easy to prepare, can be made well in advance, and will prove useful. To spend some pleasurable and productive time in the kitchen, take a few hours to make up and freeze or refrigerate one or two of these basic preparations.

APPLE CIDER REDUCTION

Reduction is the simple act of concentrating the flavor and increasing the body of a liquid by reducing the water in it. If I can claim one small addition to the practice of cuisine, this cider reduction recipe, which I developed to add thickness to vegetable stocks, would be it. I use this reduction in other ways, too: as one would use *glace de viande* (the reduced meat or fish glaze so popular in French cuisine), as a sauce, and as a superb cider syrup.

You may use either fresh pressed or fermented apple cider, but don't use apple juice, as the suspended solids in cider add necessary "weight" to the final reduction. You may also add different flavors, but never add salt, as the saltiness of the final reduction will be impossible to predict. When salt is called for later in a recipe, include it during the final cooking.

Yields
1/2 CUP (118 ML)

Note. Changing the flavor of your reduction is as easy as adding a few extra ingredients before starting the reduction process. Following are a few suggested flavors, but by all means use your imagination. The possible variations are almost limitless.

1/4 cup (59 ml) cider vinegar (for a tart reduction)

1 cinnamon stick and 2 whole cloves (for a spiced reduction)

2 sprigs thyme, 1 sprig rosemary, and 1 sprig marjoram (for an herbed reduction)

2 hot chilies, split (for a hot/spicy reduction)

3 whole coriander seeds, 1/4 teaspoon cumin, 1/4 teaspoon curry, and 1/8 teaspoon cloves (for a curried reduction)

HAVE ON HAND

2- to 3-quart (1.9 to 2.8 l) saucepan

Cheesecloth or kitchen towel

INGREDIENTS

3 cups (710 ml) fresh apple cider or fermented cider

METHOD

■ Pour the liquid (in this case, apple cider) into a saucepan that is large enough to be no more than half filled. Place the pan over high heat, and bring the liquid to a boil. Reduce the heat to medium—just high enough to maintain a very slow boil, and boil off the desired amount of water.

■ If you're using fresh, unfiltered cider, use a small ladle to skim off the foam during this slow-boil stage. To produce an especially clear reduction, when the liquid has been reduced by half, strain it through a few layers of cheesecloth or through a kitchen towel and into a clean saucepan before resuming.

■ How much liquid should you boil away? For all the recipes in this book that call for a cider reduction, the final reduction should be as thick as maple syrup. (As a matter of fact, this is exactly how maple syrup is made.) How long you'll need to cook the cider will depend on the amount of sugar in it. In most cases, 3 cups (710 ml) of cider will need to be cooked down to about 1/2 cup (118 ml).

■ Remove the pan from the heat, and allow the contents to cool. The reduction will keep for months if it's stored in a sterile sealed jar. Refrigerate the jar after opening.

CIDER VERJUS

Verjus is an ancient recipe, the basic ingredient of which is very tart fruit juice, usually grape or apple. The recipe provided here is an adaptation of one from a mentor of mine, Madeleine Kamman. As you'll see, it's very potent—so potent that I've named one dish that I make with it "Vegetables Struck by Lightning" (a reference to the "white lightning" I used to concoct a particularly excellent batch of verjus). Use this verjus sparingly in your cooking!

Yields
APPROXIMATELY 12 CUPS (2.8 L)

Note: In the recipes in this book, you may substitute cider verjus for vinegar.

HAVE ON HAND

1-gallon (3.8 l) glass jar

Cheesecloth

INGREDIENTS

4 cups (.9 l) fresh apple cider

2/3 cup (158 ml) honey (sourwood preferred)

8 cups (1.9 l) 90-proof grain alcohol

2 cups (473 ml) sherry vinegar

4 tart apples, quartered and seeds removed

METHOD

■ Strain the cider. In a large glass jar, combine all the ingredients except the apples. Stir well to dissolve the honey. Add the apples, and cover the mouth of the jar with several layers of cheesecloth. Set aside for 1 to 2 months.

■ The verjus is ready when the apples have dropped to the bottom of the jar and the liquid is clear. Carefully ladle or siphon the clear liquid from the sediment, and store in tightly capped bottles. The verjus will keep for several years.

RED-ONION-and-APPLE PURÉE

This basic preparation came to me from Joe Trull, who worked in my kitchen for a few years. The recipe has many uses, as you'll discover when you read the recipe on pages 40–41. If refrigerated, the purée will keep for several weeks.

Yields
ABOUT 6 CUPS (1.4 L)

HAVE ON HAND

11" x 16" x 4" (27.9 x 40.6 x 10.2 cm) roasting pan

Food processor or blender

INGREDIENTS

1 cup (230 g) butter

3 medium red onions, peeled and quartered

10 medium apples (combine two varieties)

Juice and zest of 2 lemons

1 teaspoon fresh ginger, peeled and sliced

1 teaspoon cardamom

1 tablespoon brown sugar

4 tablespoons Calvados (apple brandy)

1 tablespoon honey

METHOD

■ Preheat the oven to 350°F (177°C). Cut up the butter, place it in the roasting pan, and melt it, either on top of the stove over medium heat or in the oven. Then add all the ingredients except the Calvados and honey. Toss well to coat with butter, and place the pan in the oven.

■ Roast for about 2 hours, turning the mixture every 20 minutes, until the apples and onions are well browned and very soft. Remove the roasting pan from the oven, add the Calvados and honey, and purée the contents in a food processor or blender. Cool and refrigerate until ready to use.

APPLE *and* LEEK STOCK

This recipe yields a thick apple and vegetable stock. I developed it as I was trying to figure out a flavorful vegetable-based stock to use as a foundation in my cooking—one that would make use of local ingredients, that would satisfy my own taste preferences, which tend toward fruity flavors, and that would have a broad application in my cuisine.

Of all the basic recipes that the good cook uses, there's no substitute for an excellent stock, whether meat, fish, or vegetable. The technique described here can be applied to any type of stock you make.

Yields
APPROXIMATELY 1 GALLON (3.8 L)

Notes: In all cuisines, the art of making a fine stock is considered to be one of the foundations of excellence. Even with years of cooking experience behind me, I'm still an avid student of stock making. Careful execution of details and attention to the helpful tricks listed below can transform your cooking from the ordinary to the sublime.

Make about 3 or 4 gallons (11.4 or 15.1 l) of stock at a time. The stock can be reduced, frozen in ice-cube trays, and then stored in sealed, plastic freezer bags. When you need some stock, simply remove the cubes from the freezer, and add a little water if necessary.

Use the freshest ingredients. No amount of technique will rescue tired vegetables or old meat. (If you plan to make a meat-based stock, save bones in the freezer. As a rule of thumb, the amount of vegetables in your stock should equal the amount of bones.) Remember, too, that ingredient amounts aren't as important as ingredient ratios. Too much celery, for example, makes a stock bitter; too many onions make it sour; and too many carrots make it too sweet.

To enhance the flavor of the stock, brown the vegetables (and meat, if any) by roasting them slowly in a preheated oven. Coat the vegetables with a little oil, and roast at 350°F (177°C), until well browned. (This may take a few hours.) Turn the ingredients frequently to brown them evenly.

Start with just enough cold liquid (water, cider, or wine, for example) to barely cover the ingredients in your stockpot. Then bring the temperature up slowly, and cook the stock slowly, too. Rapid boiling makes cloudy, bitter stock, which is impossible to correct later. The heat under the stock should be just high enough to maintain a slow simmer; watch for tiny bubbles.

Skim the surface of the stock frequently, removing any scum that rises to the top.

Store your stocks under the most sanitary of conditions. If you refrigerate a stock for more than 3 or 4 days, reboil it before using. The reason broths are so healthy to eat is because they're rich in concentrated nutrients—the same nutrients that feed the simpler organisms of the world!

Do not add any salt to your stocks while they are cooking. Salt should be added to the recipe in which you use the stock.

HAVE ON HAND

2-gallon (7.6 l) stockpot

Roasting pan, 11" x 16" x 4" (27.9 x 40.6 x 10.2 cm) or larger

INGREDIENTS

6 leeks, with the top quarter removed, split in half, washed, and cut into 1" (2.5 cm) pieces

2 large yellow onions, cut into quarters

8 medium apples, cut into quarters, seeds removed

4 stalks of celery, washed and cut into 1" (2.5 cm) pieces

4 medium carrots, washed and cut into 1" (2.5 cm) pieces

1/4 cup (59 ml) light cooking oil

6 sprigs of parsley

1 small bunch thyme

10 peppercorns

5 whole coriander seeds

2 pieces of cinnamon stick, 2" (5.1 cm) long

3 cups (710 ml) fresh apple cider

METHOD

■ Preheat the oven to 350°F (177°C). Place the leeks, onions, apples, celery, and carrots in the roasting pan. Toss with the cooking oil, and place in the oven. Roast for 1 to 1-1/2 hours, tossing every 20 minutes, until the vegetables are well browned and golden in color. Remove from the oven.

■ Place the vegetables in the stockpot. Add about 1 cup (237 ml) water to the roasting pan, and, using a wooden or metal spatula, loosen the little bits of vegetable and any brown juices from the bottom of the pan. Add this to the stockpot.

■ Add the remaining ingredients, along with just enough water to cover the vegetables. Bring the stock to a simmer over medium heat; this will take about 1 hour. Adjust the heat to keep the stock at a simmer, partially cover the pot with a lid, and simmer for 6 to 8 hours. Strain and discard the vegetables. Cool and refrigerate the stock.

APPLESAUCE *and* APPLE BUTTER

As you make applesauce or apple butter, keep in mind that the more acidic the apples you use, the easier it will be to cook them down to a fine purée. Applesauce can be chunky, of course; whether it is or not will depend both on the acidity of your apples and the length of time that you cook the sauce.

The benchmark of culinary apples is the Bramley's Seedling, an apple that dates back to the early nineteenth century farm of Miss Mary Anne Brailsford. Because the Bramley's is so acidic, it cooks to a very fine purée.

Yields
3 CUPS (710 ML) OF APPLESAUCE OR APPLE BUTTER

Notes: The major difference between applesauce and apple butter is that apple butter has a much higher proportion of cider to apples—often 1 gallon (3.8 l) of cider to 1 pound (454 g) of apples.

One pound (454 g) of apples will make about 1-1/2 cups (355 ml) of applesauce.

Skins, which will add flavor and color to applesauce, may be removed or left on the fruit. (Do remove them when making apple butter.) Some apple skins cook down; others remain chewy, even after lengthy cooking. It's wise to select apple varieties known to make good applesauce, but almost any variety can be used.

HAVE ON HAND

2- to 3-quart (1.9 to 2.8 l) heavy-bottomed saucepan

APPLESAUCE INGREDIENTS

8 medium apples, peeled (optional), cored, and chopped

3/4 cup (177 ml) fresh apple cider or water

Lemon juice, sugar, cinnamon and other spices (optional)

APPLE BUTTER INGREDIENTS

4 medium apples, peeled, cored, and chopped

1 gallon (3.8 l) apple cider

APPLESAUCE

METHOD

■ Place the apples in the saucepan. Add one-half of the cider or water. Bring to a simmer over medium heat. Reduce the heat to low. Cook, stirring frequently and adding the remaining liquid, until the apples become sauce. Add sugar or spices, if desired, and lemon juice if the apples taste bland. Remove from the heat.

■ For instructions on canning applesauce, turn to page 163. Uncanned applesauce will last for up to one month in the refrigerator.

APPLE BUTTER

METHOD

■ Place the apples in the saucepan, and pour one-half of the cider over them. Bring to a simmer over medium heat. Reduce the heat to low and continue to cook, stirring occasionally to prevent sticking. Add cider as needed, and continue to cook (and stir) for 3 to 4 hours. Remove from the heat. The apple butter may either be canned or kept refrigerated for up to one month.

From FANTASY to APPLESAUCE:

Apples are the easiest of fruit trees for the amateur gardener to grow—and the most rewarding. In fact, the most difficult task that the beginner faces isn't caring for the orchard but planning it. As you do the legwork, just remember that the time you spend on preparation will provide generations of enjoyment.

Planting a Backyard Orchard

Once you've made the decision to plant, you'll need to consider five important factors: the size of your orchard, where to locate it, which cultivars to plant, which rootstocks to use, and how to manage and care for the trees. Each of these choices is related to the others, and each will affect your harvest.

ORCHARD SIZE AND DESIGN

The purpose of a small backyard orchard is to provide a variety of high-quality apples that will meet your specific needs. Unless you own a vast estate and have plenty of paid labor on hand, you'll probably want to keep your orchard small.

The amount of space you'll need will depend on a number of factors, including how many trees (and apples) you'd like and which rootstocks you choose: standard, semi-dwarf, or dwarf. Before you make your decisions, take a look at the chart that follows.

ROOTSTOCK	HEIGHT	PRODUCTION
DWARF TREE	6' to 8' (1.8 to 2.4 m)	1 bushel or 45 pounds (20.4 kg)
SEMI-DWARF	9' to 15' (2.7 to 4.6 m)	5 bushels or 225 pounds (102 kg)
STANDARD	up to 40' (up to 12.2 m)	up to 30 bushels or 1350 pounds (.6 metric tons)

If you're interested in making cider, keep in mind that 1 bushel of apples will yield two to three gallons (7.6 to 11.4 l) of cider.

So where does the backyard orchard fit in? Generally speaking, standard size trees are really too big for the amateur orchardist.

While dwarf trees make wonderful additions to decorative landscaping and do provide fruit, they require intensive management. Six to twelve trees on semi-dwarfing rootstock will provide plenty of apples for eating, cooking, and cider making without creating more work than you can handle on your own.

You'll find it easiest to plan a medium-density orchard, with semi-dwarf trees spaced 10' (3 m) apart, in rows 20' (6.1 m) apart. Six trees can occupy a 20' x 20' (6.1 x 6.1 m) grid, and twelve tress will fit into a 30' x 40' (91. x 12.2 m) grid.

To prevent soil erosion on slopes, you may need to contour the rows. And while north-to-south rows will give maximum exposure to sunlight, planting parallel to the prevailing winds will prevent leaning or lop-sided trees. Taking accurate measurements at the site itself will help you consider all the factors involved.

SELECTING A SITE

The success of your orchard will be intimately linked to where you locate the trees. Of course, you may not find a site that meets all the requirements discussed in this section, but do aim for the best site available.

ACCESSIBILITY

Situate your orchard close to your home. Dragging tools and bushel baskets filled with ripe apples to and from a remote orchard site won't be any fun. A nearby site will not only save you time and energy, but will allow you to enjoy the orchard's beauty. Remember, too, the old maxim: "Out of sight, out of mind." You aren't likely to care for your orchard if it can't send you visible reminders of its needs.

TOPOGRAPHY

Gently rolling hillsides with southern exposures are the best orchard sites because they encourage good water and air drainage. Very flat terrain affords poor drainage and may be more prone to frost. Steep slopes and rough terrain may make it impossible to maneuver your lawn mower or tractor around the trees, and will make pruning and harvest difficult.

TEMPERATURE RANGES

Spring apple blossoms often die when faced with extremely cold temperatures, so avoid low-lying areas that will trap cold air. This is especially important in areas where late spring frosts are a problem. Avoid hilltop sites, too, as excessive heat can damage your apples. The ideal site is one in which air circulates freely.

SUNLIGHT

The location of your orchard, the varieties you select, how close together you plant the trees, the pruning system you use, and the local weather will all influence how much sunlight is available to your orchard. As a rule of thumb, aim for as much sunlight as possible. An orchard that faces south, with rows running north to south, works well.

WATER AND DRAINAGE

New seedlings require watering, so be sure that your orchard is either close to your household water system or to a water source of its own. Hauling water by hand is an experience worth skipping.

Unless you can afford an irrigation system, your best bet is to locate the orchard in soil that is as close to perfect as possible.

SOIL

Apple trees require well-drained and well-aerated silt-loam soils, 4' to 5' (1.2 to 3.7 m) deep. Heavy clay soils will either prevent water from penetrating to tree roots or will retain so much water that roots become waterlogged. Excessively coarse and sandy soils will drain too quickly.

One way to test the composition and drainage capabilities of your soil is to dig several 2'-deep (61 cm) holes at the selected site. Grasp some of the topsoil firmly in one fist. If it clumps into a hard ball, the soil contains a lot of clay. If it doesn't retain its shape at all, the soil is too sandy.

Fill the hole with water, and watch to see how quickly it drains away. If the water disappears almost immediately, your soil is too coarse and sandy. Add plenty of composted organic matter well before planting. If you're still staring at a hole filled with muddy water 20 minutes later, you'll want to install drainage tiles, add sand and plenty of organic matter, or choose another site.

A *Reason* TO *Plant*

Eighty percent of the apples grown in the United States consist of only eight varieties—ones which keep well, look good, and are profitable for their growers: Rome Beauty, McIntosh, Red and Golden Delicious, Jonathan, Stayman, York, and Granny Smith. While there's nothing wrong with these apples, there are hundreds more varieties available—apples that may not keep well, or that can't be polished to a blinding red color, but which taste superb.

Although devoted orchardists are working to preserve and market antique varieties, bushel baskets filled with ripe antique apples are not always easy to find. Tailgate and farmer's markets are one good source, as are "U-pick" orchards, but if you want a reliable source of truly tasty apples, your best bet is to grow your own.

Either test your soil before finalizing your site selection (testing kits are widely available), or arrange to have this done for you by your local agricultural extension agent or a private testing company. Tests are best administered in the autumn. The results may include recommendations as to the amendments your soil needs.

A soil test will measure the soil's pH—the balance between its acidity and alkalinity levels. The pH is important because it affects the ability of your trees to make use of nutrients in the soil. Apple trees prefer neutral to slightly acid soils in the 6.0 to 6.5 range.

Adjusting soil pH isn't difficult. To make alkaline soil more acid, add either powdered sulphur or acidic organic materials such as oak leaf and pine mulch. To "sweeten" soil that is too acidic, add calcium carbonate, more commonly known as lime. Dolomitic limestone provides magnesium as well, but if your soil already contains enough magnesium, calcitic limestone will do the job.

Add soil amendments well before planting, no later than the previous fall. Don't overdo them, either; planting seedlings in heavily amended soil can encourage young trees to grow too vigorously.

SELECTING YOUR TREES

Typically, first-time apple growers order trees on a whim—because they want to plant "something." While it's possible to start a backyard orchard on impulse, your chances of success will increase exponentially if you resist your impulses long enough to select varieties and rootstocks carefully.

ROOTSTOCKS

Before grafting was discovered, people propagated apple trees by digging roots from wild saplings or by using the plants that germinated in cider-mill pomace heaps. Today, all modern orchards and nurseries propagate their trees by grafting a scion from the parent tree onto a rootstock, so you'll need to make not one, but two selections for every tree you purchase: the variety of apple you want, and the variety of rootstock you want it to grow on. Each rootstock (and there are several) will influence the tree in particular ways, including its size and vigor, pest and disease resistance, bearing age, anchorage, and tendency toward suckering (the production of unwanted branches).

Dwarfing rootstocks tend to be brittle, so dwarf trees usually need the extra support of permanent staking. In addition, as the size of the root system decreases, the need for high-quality soil increases. If you decide to grow dwarf trees, do make sure that your soil is up to the job.

Interstem rootstocks are also available. These consist of a dwarfing interstem, which is grafted between a more vigorous rootstock and the cultivar. In this manner, the rootstock can be selected to improve anchorage in the soil without sacrificing the advantages of smaller trees. For help making wise decisions, consult with your local extension agent or nurseryman.

APPLE VARIETIES

Tens of thousands of apple varieties exist worldwide. Treat the task of choosing from among them as an adventure of discovery, and by all means taste as you deliberate. There's no substitute for experience; find and taste as many different apple varieties as you can.

In one respect, commercial growers have an easier time making selections than backyard gardeners do. They know exactly what they're looking for—high-yielding varieties that keep well, of

course, but varieties which are also disease-resistant and which will yield apples attractive to the consumer—apples that are uniform in color and size. Unfortunately, the apple varieties that meet these requirements sometimes lack flavor. As a backyard gardener, you have one distinct advantage: You can afford to consider relatively low-yielding antique or local apple varieties, the flavors of which may be exquisite.

Taste is only one element to consider as you select trees for your orchard. If you consume most of your apples fresh, select varieties that are delicious before they're cooked and that store well. If you love to cook, be sure to include apples best suited for culinary use, both sauce apples, which turn into purée quickly, and pie apples, which hold their shape when cooked. If making cider appeals to you, add a few cider varieties.

Some home orchardists use a thematic approach, selecting only local varieties, for example, or varieties that were best known during a particular time period. Others plant strictly culinary orchards, or ones that yield only red-fleshed or green-skinned fruit. You may want an orchard that yields fruit for cider making only, or one that yields apples suitable for many purposes. The choices are entirely yours.

As your search narrows, be sure to select apples that will grow well in your region. Local cultivars grown in seedling orchards have adapted to their environments and will require less intensive care. Don't limit yourself to the best-known nurseries when you order your trees, either. Investigate local sources as well.

No single formula for selection will work for every orchard—or for every individual—but if you want an all-purpose orchard that maintains its beauty throughout the growing season, use the suggestions that follow.

■ Apple blossoms must be cross-pollinated, so unless your site is close to another orchard, be sure to purchase at least two different varieties of apples, both of which blossom at the same time.

CONTINUED ON PAGE 143

HOW *Apple Trees* ARE *Propagated*

A healthy, standard-size tree will have more than 50,000 blossoms, grouped together in bunches of five or six on short stems called *fruiting spurs*. Each blossom contains both male and female parts, but because most apple trees reject their own pollen, the female portions of the blossoms must be fertilized by pollen from other apple trees. Why is it, then, that the apples on a single tree all look and taste alike? One would think that the fruit would bear the characteristics of both trees involved in its development.

The fleshy portion of an apple develops from the female part of the blossom, and its genetic characteristics come from the parent tree. The seeds, however, bear the genetic characteristics of both the tree on which the apple grew and the tree from which the pollen came. If you plant apple seeds, you'll get a tree—and apples—that combine the characteristics of both "parent" trees. What's more, even two seeds grown from the same two parent trees will be different, as there are thousands of different ways in which the genetic material of the parents can combine.

In order to propagate apple trees of the same variety, a portion of the parent tree (or *cultivar*) must be developed into a new tree. The most practical way to do this is by grafting a bit of the parent tree (known as a *scion*) onto a root system (or *rootstock*). The rootstock will influence a number of the tree's characteristics, including how large it becomes and the age at which it will bear fruit, but the scion will determine the characteristics of the fruit.

Before your select trees, decide what you want to do with the apples from your orchard. Do you imagine pantry shelves lined with luscious, canned applesauce? Do you taste the crisp, sweet flavor of a bite of fresh apple? Do you prefer tart apples or sweet ones? Do you suddenly thirst for fresh cider? Apple varieties differ widely; it would be a shame to start out with an apple that's best for eating fresh if what you crave is a slice of bread slathered with homemade apple butter. The chart that starts on page 9 provides information on a few of the thousands of apple varieties available.

Selecting the right nursery can be very important, especially if you're planning to plant old varieties. A reputable nursery will have selected the correct rootstock for each variety and will certify the rootstocks as virus free. Your local extension agent and orchardists in your area can assist you in the choice of a nursery.

Consider purchasing from a local nursery or from ones where the growing conditions are similar to your own, as these nurseries are most likely to sell varieties that will do well where you live.

If you use out-of-town nurseries, help them help you by providing them with some information: the average rainfall in your area, minimum and maximum temperatures, and chill factors. In the United States, this information is available through your local agricultural extension office. When you place your order, let your grower know when you expect delivery, and be prepared for it. Amend your soil and dig the planting holes in advance. Your trees should be planted as soon as possible after they arrive.

Apple trees may be ordered as one-year-old saplings or—from some nurseries—as bench grafts, which consist of a newly-attached root system and scion. Planting saplings is fairly straightforward; instructions are provided on page 143. *Bench grafts*, however, must be planted in a pot or in a temporary garden spot for one season before relocating them to their permanent sites. The advantages to bench grafts are that more varieties are offered, and they're relatively inexpensive. Their disadvantages are that they require more care and aren't usually guaranteed. If you anticipate instituting a grafting program of your own, experience with bench grafts will prove helpful later.

- In order to extend your apple season, select varieties that will ripen at different times.

- For a variety of flavors and uses, select three dessert varieties; three cider varieties (two for sugar/acid balance and one for tannin content); and culinary varieties for the remainder.

- Plant a crabapple in the orchard. It will pollinate your other apple trees, and its fruit can be used in cider and in jelly.

PLANTING

Ideally, you should start preparing your site two to three years before planting by correcting soil deficiencies, installing irrigation if necessary, and establishing contours and water diversions. Purchasing trees before you've prepared the orchard soil is a certain recipe for disaster!

Apple trees may be planted in the spring or fall; ask your local

growers for advice specific to your region. Fall planting allows the root system to settle in before the first spurt of spring growth.

Your trees will arrive either bare-rooted or with their roots buried in a burlap-wrapped ball of soil. Place bare-rooted trees in a slurry of topsoil and water right away, and water the tops of the trees as well. Water the roots of balled trees through the burlap until you're ready to plant.

If you're planting semi-dwarf trees, you'll need to dig holes that are each 4' (1.2 m) deep and 4' (1.2 m) wide. Start by placing a canvas tarp or heavy blanket on one side of the hole site. Position your wheelbarrow or garden cart on the other. As you

dig, place the turf and the richest soil onto the tarp, and the rocks and hardpan in the wheelbarrow or cart for disposal. Mix any necessary soil amendments, including topsoil, with the topsoil you removed.

Apple trees should be planted slightly deeper than they were in their nursery settings but not so deep that their root systems drown or so deep that the grafted scions put down root systems of their own. Interstem grafts must be a certain distance above ground level; request correct planting depths when you order them.

Shovel enough mixed topsoil into the hole to hold the tree at the proper height. Place the tree in the hole, and carefully spread out the roots of bare-rooted trees, clipping clean any that are broken. Fill the hole with soil, packing it firmly around the tree. Then slowly water the area around the roots, wiggling the tree as you do to help settle the soil and free any trapped air. (A well-prepared hole and planted tree will take an hour's worth of slow watering without any runoff.)

After watering, repack the soil lightly, and form a dike around the trunk, about 16" (40.6 cm) in diameter to help to hold moisture around the root system. No fertilizer is necessary at this point.

Before planting balled trees, snip the strings that hold the burlap covering, and carefully remove the burlap. Shovel dirt into the hole until the graft union on the tree will be held at the correct height above the ground. Fill the hole with amended topsoil, and proceed as for bare-rooted trees.

To stake newly-planted trees, cover a length of heavy wire with a short section of old garden hose. Place the stake on the upwind side of the tree, and secure it to the tree with the wire, locating the hose-covered section next to the trunk.

New trees should be pruned of the previous year's growth. Cut growth shoots back to mid-bud, and remove any excess or crossed branches. Make the cuts clean and close to the trunk and diagonal to the bud.

In northern areas where winter sunscald is a problem, paint the tree trunks white with a rubber-based paint to help reflect sunlight and reduce injury. To protect the trees from mice and rabbits, surround each trunk with a fine-meshed hardware cloth sleeve, which should extend from 2" (5.1 cm) below the soil surface to just below the first branch. White plastic, spiral tree guards, which serve as protection against both wildlife and sunscald, are also available.

For the first several months of their lives, be sure that each tree receives 10 gallons (38 l) of water per week.

ORCHARD MANAGEMENT

Day-to-day and season-to-season care of the trees you've planted includes pruning, orchard floor management, a feeding program, and pest and disease control methods. For the home orchardist, a low-tech, organic program is entirely possible. You'll end up sacrificing some apples to bugs and birds, but maximum efficiency probably won't be as important to you as it is to commercial growers. An organic management program involves more work, of course. You'll need to monitor insects, pests, and diseases carefully, and using organic controls can be time consuming.

TRAINING AND PRUNING

While teaching the fine art of pruning isn't within the scope of this book, you'll find that the information in this section gets you off to a good start. Visit your local library, and contact gardeners and orchardists in your area for more information.

In order to establish a beautiful, productive orchard for food and pleasure, you'll need to "train" or shape your trees for a three-year period after planting. Start the first spring after planting (even for trees planted that same spring), after the danger of severe freezing has passed.

Shaping a tree affects its productivity, the ripening of its fruit, and the amount of effort required to maintain the orchard in later years. Proper training establishes the correct number of bearing limbs and their placement on the tree, and maximizes sunlight penetration. Training also establishes the angle of the lateral bearing limbs, which affects the health and strength of the mature tree.

While there are many ways to shape apple trees (including bush, cordon, central leader, pyramid, standard, half-standard, and espalier), the most convenient shapes for home gardeners are the pyramid and central leader systems.

Pyramid trees, in which the upper branches are progressively shorter than those below, place less demand than many other shapes on limited garden space. Their fruit-bearing branches are exposed to sunlight, they bear fruit earlier, and the apples are relatively easy to harvest.

Central leader training creates one central "trunk," off of which two to four "platforms" or scaffolds of four to six branches each are developed. Most of the fruit is borne by the lower scaffolds with the upper branches bearing a little fruit and producing some shade.

Once the tree's shape has been established, you'll prune your trees annually, in the winter or summer, to encourage maximum fruit production and grace of shape. Pruning also assures

adequate light penetration; fruiting spurs must receive at least three to four hours of full sunlight a day.

Winter pruning removes dead and diseased wood and maintains the tree shape by removing badly placed branches. It also stimulates growth, but discourages fruit production. Summer pruning, on the other hand, which is usually used only on closely trained shapes such as pyramid, cordon, and espalier, reduces the number of leaves and restricts growth, but lets in more sunlight, encourages the formation of fruit spurs, and aids in the ripening and color development of the fruit.

Without adequate pruning, the tree will be filled with tangled growth, will produce small apples, and is likely to be unhealthy, as neglect contributes to attacks from pests and diseases. Even a neglected orchard, however, can often be brought back to health by pruning.

CLEANLINESS

Not surprisingly, the health of the orchard is directly related to its cleanliness. Weeding, raking leaves, mulching the orchard floor, and burning dead wood contribute as much to your orchard's health as any other management practice. Raking leaves from the orchard floor, for example, exposes the soil to a good winter frost, which in turn controls the apple sawfly caterpillars that can ruin your fruit in early summer. A heavy mulch will not only conserve moisture during the growing season, but will also help to prevent powdery mildew—one cause of blossom drop, which results in no fruit.

FEEDING

Depending on the site and management system you've selected, you'll also need to choose a method of providing the proper nutrients to your apple trees. While apple trees are robust, they don't tolerate marginal soil well and do need to be fed. A good soil test can guide you in determining the nutritional needs of your trees.

When adding amendments after planting, avoid chemical fertilizers and fresh manure, especially in the spring, as these will burn the roots of newly planted trees.

PESTS AND DISEASES

Although they aren't especially demanding to grow, apple trees aren't immune to pests and diseases. Common orchard pests include aphids, codling moth caterpillars, and apple suckers. Diseases such as scab, fire blight, powdery mildew, and canker affect the overall health of the trees.

While the commercial grower is usually dependent upon a very intensive pruning and chemical management system, the amateur grower can rely on more natural approaches. One of these

is the Integrated Pest Management (IMP) program, which favors the use of products such as Japanese beetle traps, apple maggot red spheres, pheromone lures, and sticky traps to control many orchard pests.

Peter Hatch, the Director of Gardens and Grounds at Monticello (Charlottesville, Virginia), has worked for the past seventeen years to restore Thomas Jefferson's gardens. Peter reminded me that with few exceptions, the fruits we grow in our North American orchards and gardens are foreign to the North American continent. Peaches, pears, plums, figs, olives, and many apples were originally imported from other lands.

As Peter has pointed out, our national infatuation with plants and plant variety has created thousands of fruit choices for the home gardener, but the fact that these plants aren't indigenous means that they're more vulnerable to pests and diseases. Careful selection of cultivars, rootstocks, and an orchard site can help to minimize the necessity for intervention, but no orchard will be perfect without any intervention at all.

Orchard sprays can consist of pure water, combinations of chemicals, or botanical materials. Whether or not you choose to use chemical sprays will be affected by your orchard location, choice of rootstock, and management methods. Some locations are less susceptible to pests than others, and some rootstocks and scions are more resistant to pests and disease.

Botanical sprays available to organic growers include rotenone (made from the roots of tropical plants), which controls insects by slowing their metabolism; pyrethrum (derived from the chrysanthemum), which is one of the shortest lived and safest insecticides and one to which insects do not develop a tolerance; and ryania (from a Latin American shrub), which is effective in the control of the coddling moth and the apple aphid. Lime, sulphur, and copper sprays are also available. The drawback to these natural sprays is that they are short-lived, so frequent applications are necessary.

Every spray is timed to the blossoming of the individual tree or variety. Different varieties blossom at different times, often over a period of a month or so; they're treated individually until all the blossom petals have fallen, after which time the orchard is treated as a whole.

Spray manufacturer's include instructions with their products, but the information that follows will give you an idea of a typical spraying schedule:

STAGE	PEST OR DISEASE	WHEN TO SPRAY
GREEN TIP	Apple scab; mildew	*When green tips first appear on buds and before the first rainfall*
PRE-PINK	Apple scab; mildew; aphids	*When blossom buds first show pink*
PINK	Apple scab; mildew; winter moths; green fruitworms	*Just before the blossoms open*
OPEN BLOSSOM		*Do not spray*
CALYX	Scab; mildew; aphids	*After all petals have fallen*
FIRST COVER	Scab; insects	*One week after calyx*
SECOND COVER	Scab; coddling moths	*10 days after first cover*
THIRD COVER	Scab; coddling moths; mites; apple maggots	*10 days after second cover*
FOURTH COVER	Apple maggots	*10 days after third cover*
FIFTH COVER	Apple maggots	*10 days later*

Stop spraying two to four weeks prior to harvest.

Several species of wildlife, including deer, rabbits, and voles, can wreak havoc in your orchard. Complete control isn't possible, but minimizing the effects is.

Protect young trees from deer and rabbits by surrounding them with tree guards or wire-mesh cylinders; the latter also offer some protection again voles. To repel deer, hang small bags of human hair or commercial repellents in the trees, replacing them after each rain. The best method for controlling voles, which attack the lateral roots of mature trees, is trapping them.

To control deer and rabbits at Monticello, Thomas Jefferson built a "paling" fence, nearly 3/4 of a mile (1.21 km) long, around his orchard and garden. This fence consisted of thin boards, 10' (3 m) high, placed "so near as not to let even a young hare in." Fencing the orchard is a realistic option for the small home orchardist.

Other methods of control exist, including heavy netting placed over the trees to prevent bird damage, but these methods are often expensive and time consuming.

HARVEST

Newly planted trees won't bear at all for the first two years and will yield only a small crop during the third. By the fourth year, each tree should bear about 1/2 bushel (10.2 kg); by the fifth year, 2 bushels (40.8 kg); and by the sixth year, you can expect 5 bushels (102 kg) annual production from a semi-dwarf tree. As you now know, however, many variables will effect the success of your orchard. Fruit production is never a certainty.

Even fruit for cider making is better when it's picked or shaken from the tree. Among the tools that make this task easier is the fruit hook, which is nothing more than a long pole with a small hook on its end. Another is the harvest blanket, a large canvas cloth that is wrapped around the base of the tree and that stretches out beyond the perimeter of the branches. The outer edges of the blanket are raised slightly. When the apples fall, they roll toward the blanket's center, preventing injury to the fruit and smearing with dirt.

REAPING THE REWARDS

There's nothing quite as exhilarating as the first bite from an apple that you've grown yourself. You'll forget the blisters you suffered after digging holes for your new trees, the panic you endured the first time you encountered aphids, the irritation that swept over you when you realized you might have to share your harvest with feathered invaders. In fact, you're likely to forget everything except the apple in your hand and its sweet, tangy flavor in your mouth.

Orchard Tools AND Materials

Caring for your backyard orchard will be more of a pleasure than a chore if you own or can borrow the right tools. The list that follows includes the basics, although many others are available.

Square-edged garden shovel
Heavy four-prong garden fork
Wheelbarrow or garden cart, for moving trees, dirt, tools, and harvested apples.
10' x 10' (3 x 3 m) heavy canvas tarp, on which to place dirt dug from holes
Roto-tiller (not essential, but can be helpful if you need to add soil amendments)
Heavy hammer, for pounding in garden stakes
Buckets, for soaking bare-rooted tree roots before planting
Tree stakes, strong wire, and 6" (15.2 cm) sections of old garden hose to serve as supports for new trees
Tree wrap and tree guards, for protecting the trees from wildlife and sunscald
Pocket knife with a sharp blade, for a variety of tasks
Long-handled clippers, for most pruning tasks
Fine-toothed saw, for cutting larger branches
Hand clippers, for pruning smaller shoots
Grafting/pruning wax, to protect cut surfaces
1/2" (1.3 cm) brush, for applying pruning wax
Fruit hook, for detaching ripe fruit from the trees
Harvest blanket on which to gather apples

HARVEST PICNIC

Across cultures and for thousands of years, the harvest season has been a time of gratitude and joy. In celebration of the completion of this book, and the hundreds of apples that were harvested and eaten as the recipes in it were created, my friends and I gathered for an outdoor apple feast. Most of the dishes (recipes for which are listed at the end of this section) were variations on traditional North American harvest-time dishes that have been enjoyed for more than two hundred years.

The apple orchards at historic Hickory Nut Gap Farm in Fairview, North Carolina, where we played, ate, and strolled, belong to Jamie and Elspeth McClure Clark, who, with the help of their daughter Annie Ager, grow and sell their own apples and cider to people from far and near. We couldn't have selected a more scenic picnic site or more gracious hosts.

ABOVE: MARK SLICES HAM FOR THE HUNGRY GUESTS.

RIGHT: THE HARVEST PICNIC. TWENTY MINUTES LATER, THE TABLE WAS BARE.

BELOW: A WELL-TRAINED GUEST AWAITS HIS SHARE.

LOWER RIGHT: ONE OF THE GUESTS BROUGHT ALONG AN APPLE-CINNAMON SYRUP FOR THE GROUP TO SAMPLE.

UPPER LEFT: AUTHOR MARK ROSENSTEIN WITH PHOTOGRAPHER EVAN BRACKEN

RIGHT: MARK SAMPLES HIS STONE FENCE PUNCH.

LEFT: ART DIRECTOR DANA IRWIN TOOK THE DAY OFF TO ACT AS MEAL AND SOCIAL DIRECTOR.

OTHERS: A FEW OF THE PICNIC GUESTS

HARVEST RECIPES

Cider-Cured Country Ham (pages 72–73)

Loin of Venison with An Apple and Dried Cherry Crust (pages 70–71)

Pork Tenderloin Served in the Style of a Good Housewife (pages 74–75)

Roasted Capon with Apple Butter (pages 78–79)

October Cider Beans (pages 76–77)

Braised Leeks, Apples, and Napa Cabbage with Sweet Spice (pages 98–99)

Apple Bread (pages 26–27)

Susie's Applesauce (page 87)

Apples and Sauerkraut (page 96)

Apple Horseradish Sauce (pages 94–95)

Indian Apple Pudding (page 103)

Apple Leather (pages 130–131)

Pumpkin and Apple Tart with Currants (pages 128–129)

Pommes a l'Eau-de-Vie (pages 24–25)

Mulled Cider (page 21)

Stone Fence Punch (page 23)

APPLE CIDER and CIDER VINEGAR

Making cider at home is an incredibly exciting adventure, one to which I'm becoming addicted and which I encourage you to try. While I won't provide complete instructions here, I'll whet your appetite by describing the general procedure.

THE DAY STARTS WITH DELIVERY OF APPLES FROM THE ORCHARD.

PREPARING TO WASH THE APPLES

The basic process is very simple. Yeast from the air converts sugar in the apple juice to carbon dioxide and alcohol. Like many simple processes, however, cider making is not always easy.

MAKING APPLE CIDER

Two ingredients are necessary: excellent juice and an unrelenting passion for cleanliness. Good cider-making juice, whether pressed from vintage cider apples or blended from a variety of apples, must have the correct balance of sugar, acid, and tannin. If you plan to make cider, it's well worth learning the following terms, as they're often used in descriptions of cider apple varieties:

BITTERSWEET: *high in tannin and sugar*

BITTERSHARP: *high in tannin and acid*

SWEET: *low in tannin, high in sugar (juicy dessert apples)*

SHARP: *low in tannin, high in acid (similar to cooking apples)*

Don't let the prospect of having to test apple juice put you off. The titration test for acid content and a sugar test performed with a hydrometer are surprisingly easy, and the necessary equipment (in fact, all the equipment for home cider making)

ABOVE AND LOWER LEFT: APPLES BEING FED INTO AN ELECTRIC GRINDING MILL

POMACE (GROUND APPLES) AWAITING PRESSING

is available at many beer- or wine-making shops, as well as at natural food stores.

High acidity levels—desirable in juice used for cider making—help prevent infection of the cider by unwanted bacteria. Good cider juice should have an acid level of .6 percent of the total volume. Apple varieties range widely in acid content, from a low of .15 percent to a high of 1.0 percent. Sugar levels determine the eventual alcohol content of the finished cider and should be between 6 and 16 percent, preferably within the 8 to 12 percent range.

While cider may be made from orchard windfalls (their appearance isn't important), excellent cider is made from apples that have been picked from the tree and that are clean and fresh. After they're harvested, apples to be pressed for premium ciders are allowed to ripen further—a process known as *mellowing* (or *sweating*). As they do, water within the fruit begins to evaporate, complex carbohydrates are converted into simple sugars, and the cell walls of the fruit grow thinner and weaker, making the release of juice more complete during pressing.

Because cider apple varieties tend to be very hard, juice extraction is usually a two-step process made up of grinding and pressing. First, the mellowed apples are hosed down or washed in a tub to remove all dirt and any residual sprays. After draining, they're ground into a pulp (or *pomace*), either by crushing them or by rasping or grating them.

The next step is pressing the juice from the pomace. In centuries past, a special form (or *cheese*) was made by layering the apples in horsehair blankets which held the pomace while the juice was pressed from it. The cheese included a pathway for the escaping juices. Today, home presses come with cheeses consisting of nylon-covered plastic trays.

Two types of small presses are available, both suitable for the home cider maker: the central screw tub press, also used for wine making; and the platen-type press, traditionally used in English cider making. The first press will work well, but a filter bag must be placed inside the tub, or the pulp will squeeze out the sides. In a platen press, the pulp is wrapped in alternating layers in a cheese consisting of a porous material such as heavy canvas or nylon. The cheese is then placed between two large flat plates to which pressure is applied by either a screw or ratchet mechanism. The juice (or *must*), which leaves the press through a channeled tray, is collected in a separate container. The must may be filtered after pressing, but today, it's usually just strained to remove the larger organic particles.

THE PRESS AS THE CHEESE IS ABOUT TO BE ASSEMBLED

CHANNELS IN THE GRAY TRAY WILL DIRECT THE JUICE AS IT RUNS OUT OF THE CHEESE.

HYDRAULIC CIDER PRESS IN ONE STAGE OF ASSEMBLY

At this stage, the must is tested for its sugar and acid content, which will vary from year to year. Adjustments are made, and then the must is placed in large vats, or—in the case of home cider makers—in a large, clean, non-reactive container such as a plastic garbage pail. The must is either sterilized by adding a little sulphur dioxide and then inoculated with a commercial yeast mixture, or left unsterilized and inoculated naturally by yeast that was on the apple skins.

Controlling the temperature of the must is critical. A slow fermentation at low temperatures usually gives the best results, so the cider container (known as the primary fermenter) is placed in a cool area such as a cellar. Temperature-controlled water baths are available, but they're expensive and not really necessary. A temperature range of between 60°F and 70°F (15°C to 21°C) is acceptable.

For the first few days, very little happens, but once fermentation gets going, the must becomes surprisingly active. An almost explosive release of gas will begin; you won't need to protect the must from air at this stage because escaping gas will push up a "cap" composed of the larger organic particles in the juice.

As the fermentation slows, and after the cap has risen, the cider is siphoned into 5-gallon (18.9 l) glass jugs known as *carboys*, and the caps are discarded. The carboys are then sealed by fastening a fermentation lock onto each one. This S-shaped tube, which is partly filled with water and fitted with a cork, permits carbon dioxide to escape from the cider, but prevents air from entering.

Once the fermenting cider is "under lock," precautions are taken to exclude air from the carboys and to keep the cider sterile. Fermentation can take from several weeks to several months. When to bottle the cider will depend on the type of cider being made.

Some cider makers transfer (or *rack*) the cider once during the fermentation process. This is usually done by siphoning the cider into clean carboys in order to separate the clear cider from the dead yeast cells and other organic matter (or *lees*) in the bottom of the old carboys. Racking isn't absolutely necessary, but it does produce a clearer cider and improves certain flavors. Its disadvantage is the danger of introducing airborne bacteria during the process. The bottles and siphoning equipment must be thoroughly sterilized.

LEFT: THE NYLON BLANKET THAT WILL HOLD THE POMACE DURING PRESSING

ABOVE: FILLING THE CHEESE WITH POMACE

RIGHT: THE PREPARED PRESS. NOTE THE FOOT-OPERATED HYDRAULIC CYLINDER UNDER IT.

CIDER MAKING ON LONG ISLAND

WILLIAM M. DAVIS
NEW YORK STATE HISTORICAL ASSOCIATION, COOPERSTOWN, NY

Settlers in North America brought with them a heritage of cider pressing. Establishing a seedling orchard was one of their first tasks after they claimed and cleared land.

In Colonial times, cider was a common drink, consumed at every hour of the day, in part because people questioned the wholesomeness of fresh water. Farmers started their days with it, physicians recommended it for good health, and even children drank fermented and diluted cider. Housewives used cider vinegar to pickle fruits and vegetables.

Cider also held a position of prominence because it was able to satisfy the colonists' desire for alcoholic beverages. European grapes didn't fare well, and native grapes made a wine deemed barely drinkable. Apples, however, not only grew well, but their juice could be fermented to make hard cider, and the cider could be distilled to make a potent apple brandy known as applejack.

In New England, by 1775, one in every ten farms operated its own cider mill. As had been the case in England earlier, cider was sometimes used as a form of currency. Farm help, doctors, and tailors were paid with cider, a contribution of cider was allotted to the preacher, and cider was applied to the cost of children's education.

New Jersey became the center of the early American cider industry. In fact, the city we know as Newark was once the site of many orchards and boasted a thriving cider industry. In Essex County in 1810, 198,000 barrels of cider were produced.

By the middle of the nineteenth century, with over 6,000 local temperance groups promoting moderation or abstinence in the United States, carbonated waters began to replace hard cider. The pressure to reform drinking habits was sometimes so strong that orchards were destroyed. Cider lovers also had to fight commercial pressures. The rise in demand for fine dessert apples, which brought higher prices to the farmer, gradually led to the disappearance of cider apples from many orchards. By the early 1900s, the word "cider" had come to mean the unfermented juice of surplus table apples.

Filtering—the process of removing any remaining undesirable particles in the finished cider—is difficult for the home cider maker to perform and not really necessary because careful racking can be used to achieve the same results.

The cider is bottled by siphoning it into sterile bottles, leaving 1/2" (1.3 cm) at the top of each one. Great care is taken to place the end of the siphon right at the bottom of the bottle so that as little air as possible will be introduced during siphoning. The bottles are sealed with stoppers or corks, allowed to rest for at least a week, and then stored in a cool, dark place to age. Bottles sealed with corks are placed on their sides in order to keep the corks moist and swollen.

As simple as the cider-making process seems, cider is a delicate beverage and is susceptible to a few common maladies. Most of these problems can be avoided by being careful and by keeping everything scrupulously clean.

Because ciders begin their life with low acid and alcohol levels, many microorganisms find them to be hospitable environments, including aerobic organisms known as acetobacters; "flowers"—greasy, ash-like films on the tops of ciders; the bacteria Zymomonas mobilis, which causes unsavory aromas; and anaerobic organisms such as lactic acid bacteria, which, while they don't affect the cider's taste, produce a ropiness that results in an unpleasant texture. The best preventive measures for all these problems are the exclusion of air and constant attention to cleanliness. Keeping the cider cool, avoiding racking when its specific gravity is between 1.025 and 1.035, making sure that its pH is below 3.7, and making sure that it doesn't sit for long on the lees or settled yeast, will all help as well.

If you decide to tackle cider making at home, don't be discouraged by early failures. Start with small batches. In time and with practice, you'll be rewarded with a beverage that is timeless in its perfection and simplicity.

MAKING CIDER VINEGAR

Cider vinegar is created when oxygen—with the help of microscopic organisms known as acetobacters—combines with the alcohol in hard cider. As the cider ferments, a jellylike mass known as the "mother of cider" or "mother" forms. This

FRESH JUICE!

COLLECTING THE PRESSED JUICE

FILTERING THE JUICE THROUGH COARSE CHEESE-CLOTH

The cider makers of old knew how to select and blend apples so that the balance of sugar, acid, and tannin would be perfect. Individual apple varieties containing a good balance—cider apples such as Foxwhelp, for example—are known as vintage cider apples; these apples needn't be blended with others to make good cider. Unfortunately, true cider apples, which are more closely related to the wild crab than to the dessert apples favored by consumers, are increasingly difficult to find.

FRENCH CIDER APPLES

Today, French cider apples and cider-making practices are the ones that remain truest to tradition. French cider makers recognize different types of cider, each distinguished by the ripening season of the fruit used (the later apples are generally higher in sugar). The "petite" ciders are made from September fruit, the "ordinaire" ciders from October fruit, and the "grande" ciders from November apples. Most French varieties are bittersweets.

Binet Blanc
Binet Rouge
Calville Blanc
Julien de Paulmier
Medaille d'Or
Marechal
Michelin
Moulin-a-Vent
Reine des Pommes
St. Laurent

ENGLISH CIDER APPLES

Many English cider apples have their roots in the French countryside, but because the English climate suited them better, their special properties became noted only after the move across the channel. Other varieties arose in England, most of them dating back to the period between the late 1700s and the mid 1800s. English varieties include the full range: sweets, sharps, bittersweets, and bittersharps.

Ashmead's Kernel
Ashton Brown Jersey
Babinett
Bulmer's Norman
Brown Snout
Cherry Norman
Chisel Jersey
Crimson King
Eggleston Styre
Foxwhelp
Major
Nonpareil
Strawberry Norman
Sweet Alford
Sweet Coppin
Tremblett's Bitter
Yarlington Mill

NORTH AMERICAN CIDER APPLES

Cider making in North America reached its peak in the early 1800s. By that time, cider varieties—many from England but even more from the seedling orchards of the New World—were well established. Few of these apples, however, were cultivated for cider alone. Of the few American apples that were strictly cider varieties, many have disappeared, perhaps forever. The Tolliver (or Talieforo) and the Harrison are two such examples.

Baldwin
Golden Russet
Graniwinkle
Gravenstein
Grimes
Hewes (or Virginia) Crab
Horse apples
Hyslop Crab
Lindel
Newtown Pippin
Northern Spy
Red Astrackan
Roxbury Russet
Smith's Cider
Stayman Winesap
Virginia Crab
Winesap

mother can be transferred and used to speed up future batches of vinegar.

Making vinegar at home isn't quite as easy as it sounds, but with care, it's certainly possible. Two warnings are in order. First, never use homemade vinegars for preserving or pickling, as their acidity levels aren't always high enough. Second, keep the cider-making and vinegar-making processes completely separate. Don't use the same equipment or space. Once a vinegar culture has been established, it's nearly impossible to eliminate, and a vinegar culture will ruin your cider-making efforts.

Before you start, gather together the following items:

■ A wide-mouthed container (glass, plastic, wood, ceramic, or enamel) twice as large as the amount of vinegar you'd like to make.

■ Several layers of cheesecloth and some string

■ Hard apple cider, preferably preservative-free, with a minimum alcohol content of not less than 5 percent. If you can't find cider without preservatives in it, pour the cider back and forth between clean containers for 5 minutes to help the preservatives dissipate. Your cider must have a relatively high acid level, and it must be completely "dry." Residual sugar will encourage the growth of molds, and low acidity leads to the growth of undesirable bacteria.

■ Vinegar bacteria. These are available for free in the air we breathe, but mothers are sometimes available from wine-making shops and mail-order sources and can be found in bottles of unpasteurized commercial vinegars.

■ A dark area in which to allow the cider to ferment. Temperatures ranging from 59°F to 86°F (15°C to 30°C) are acceptable.

FRESH APPLES NEXT TO DISCARDED POMACE

Unless you want to develop your own mother, start by pouring the cider into the wide-mouthed container and adding either a mother or 1 quart (.9 l) of unpasteurized cider vinegar to each gallon (3.8 l) of cider. Cover the mouth of the container with a few layers of cheesecloth, and use the string to tie the cloth tightly around the opening. Set the container in a dark place such as a cupboard or closet. You're most likely to face bacterial problems if you've added no finished vinegar at the start of the process and are trying to develop a mother with airborne inoculants.

The alcohol in the cider will take anywhere from two to several months to convert to vinegar. Smell and taste the vinegar periodically to make sure that it hasn't been infected with undesirable bacteria.

To develop your own mother, follow the same steps, but add nothing to the cider. As the cider ferments, airborne organisms will inoculate it. In two to four weeks, a mother will form on its own, and the vat or jar will smell distinctly of vinegar. Place a portion of the mother in a clean bottle, add a little cider to it, and set it aside for your next batch of vinegar. Allow the cider to continue fermenting.

STARTING ANOTHER BATCH

When the vinegar is ready, draw off as much as you want. Strain it through several layers of cheesecloth, and store it in clean, tightly corked bottles, filling each one to the top and using new corks to provide a good seal. If you'd like to continue producing vinegar, leave some in the container, and fill the container no more than two-thirds full with additional cider.

Cloudiness in finished vinegar is caused by the continued growth of the vinegar bacteria. There are three ways to prevent this from happening. Add ascorbic acid to each bottle, following the directions that come with the ascorbic acid; pasteurize the vinegar by heating it to 150°F (66°C); or process it in a boiling-water bath for 5 minutes (see "Canning Apple Juice" on pages 163–165). Ascorbic acid can be purchased wherever beer- or wine-making supplies are available, as well as at many health-food stores.

After you've made your first batch of vinegar and have saved a mother, making subsequent batches is even easier. Simply add a little of the reserved mother to the new cider. Once the fermentation process is underway, remove a little of the mother, and reserve it in a clean jar of fresh cider so that you'll have enough mother for the next batch.

Cider IN England

Cider was introduced to England from Normandy during the eleventh century. Before long, most monasteries had planted seedling orchards, and the monks had learned to apply their wine-making skills to apples. For the next several centuries, cider was a mainstay of life in England and figured heavily in the overall farm economy, serving as wages, barter, and food. To all but the very rich and the very poor, cider was the wine of England and for some time competed with ale as the most popular national drink.

Farmers produced cider each autumn from fruit grown in their own orchards. They drank this cider, of course, but it also served as a form of barter. As a portion of their wages, farm laborers were often given a daily ration of cider made the previous fall—usually about 1/2 gallon (1.9 liters). The cider was transferred from barrels in the farm's cider house to individual wooden bottles called firkins or costrels. Farmers who didn't make cider were likely to have a difficult time hiring temporary harvest workers.

Oddly enough, the popularity of cider in England may have impeded the development of grafted varieties in that country. By growing seedling orchards, in which every tree differed from its neighbor, farmers were guaranteed good cider blends, as they could combine varieties for their sweetness, acidity, and tannin content. Only in countries such as France, where dessert apples were more popular than cider, did growers have any compelling reason to develop single varieties that would remain true to strain.

CANNING *and* PRESERVING

*E*ven apple varieties that keep well in a cool root cellar or in the refrigerator won't usually last longer than a few months. To extend your apple-eating season, you may want to can, freeze, or dry some of your harvest.

APPLES

WATER-BATH CANNING

Apple slices, sauce, preserves, and juice may be canned in a boiling-water bath or in a pressure canner.

For water-bath canning, you'll need a canning kettle large enough to hold seven 1-quart (.9 l) jars on a rack. The kettle must be deep enough to allow each jar to be covered with 2" (5.1 cm) of water and for that water to come to a rolling boil without flooding your stove.

Remember to use only unblemished fruit. The better the apples look now, the better they will taste later—and the fewer problems you'll have with spoilage. Wash the fruit very well before peeling.

To sterilize your canning jars, first wash them, the lids, and the bands in hot, soapy water. Rinse thoroughly. Place the lids and bands in a clean pan, cover with boiling water, and leave submerged until you're ready to use them.

Carefully place the jars on the rack in the canning kettle. Pour hot water into both the jars and kettle until the water covers the jars by at least 1" (2.5 cm). Place the lid on the kettle, bring the water to a vigorous boil, and boil for 10 minutes. At altitudes of greater than 1,000' (305 m), add 1 minute for each additional 1,000'. Turn the heat down, and leave the jars in the simmering water until you're ready to pack them with fruit.

CANNING APPLE SLICES

Plan on using 3 medium apples for each 1 quart (.9 l) jar.

1.

Prepare the jars and lids as described in the "Water-Bath Canning" section.

2.

For each 1-quart (.9 l) jar to be filled, measure 2 cups (473 ml) of water and 1 cup (200 g) of extra-fine sugar into a pan. Boil slowly until the sugar has dissolved, and remove from the heat.

3.

Peel, core, and slice the clean apples. (A mechanical apple peeler will help make the first task easier.) To help prevent discoloration, submerge the slices in a solution of 2 tablespoons of lemon juice and 1 gallon (3.8 l) of water.

4.

Remove the sterilized jars from the canning kettle, and keep the remaining water at a simmer. Drain the apple slices, and fill the jars with them to within 1/2" (1.3 cm) of the top. Be careful not to crush the apple slices.

5.

Bring the syrup back to a rolling boil, and then, using a funnel, pour it over the apple slices to fill each jar to within 1/2" (1.3 cm) of its top. Run a small rubber spatula around the inside of each jar to release any air bubbles.

6.

Wipe the rims of the jars with a clean, damp towel, place a lid on each one, and twist a band down tightly over the lid. The rims must be perfectly clean, or the jars won't seal properly.

7.

Place the jars in the kettle, and add enough hot water to bring the water level to within 2" or 3" (5.1 to 7.6 cm) of its top. Place the lid on the kettle, and bring the water to a rolling boil before you start timing. Process the jars for 20 minutes in the boiling-water bath.

8.

Remove the jars from the kettle, and place them in a draft-free area to cool undisturbed for 12 to 24 hours. (Don't retighten the metal screw bands.)

9.

After the cooling period, remove the screw bands, and set aside; the bands can be re-used. Don't leave them on the jars, as they serve no useful function once the lids have sealed and are likely to rust as well.

10.

Check each lid to see that it has sealed properly. In the center of a properly sealed lid, you'll see a small, indented "dimple." If the centers are indented, wash, dry, and label the jars. If a lid

HOT-PACK PROCESSING TIMES IN BOILING-WATER BATH

Note the adjusted times for processing at certain altitudes.

CONTENTS	JAR SIZE	AT ALTITUDES OF 0 to 1,000' (0-305 m)	AT ALTITUDES OF 1,001' to 3,000' (305-914 m)
APPLE BUTTER	1/2 pints or pints (237 or 473 ml)	5 minutes	10 minutes
	Quarts (.9 l)	10 minutes	15 minutes
APPLE JUICE	Pints or quarts (473 ml or .9 l)	5 minutes	10 minutes
	1/2 gallons (1.9 l)	10 minutes	15 minutes
APPLESAUCE	Pints (473 ml)	15 minutes	20 minutes
	Quarts (.9 l)	20 minutes	25 minutes
SLICED APPLES	Pints or quarts (473 ml or .9 l)	20 minutes	25 minutes
APPLE RINGS	1/2 pints or pints (237 or 473 ml)	10 minutes	15 minutes
CRAB APPLES	Pints (473 ml)	20 minutes	25 minutes

isn't dimpled, either use the contents right away or reprocess within 24 hours. If the well-sealed jars are kept in a cool, dark, dry place, the apples may be eaten for up to one year.

CANNING APPLESAUCE

One bushel of apples (approximately 45 pounds or 20.4 kg) will make between 16 and 20 quarts (15.1 and 18.9 l) of applesauce.

1.

Wash, peel, quarter, and core the apples. (Depending on the apple variety, peeling may be unnecessary.)

2.

Make the applesauce, following the basic instructions on page 135. You'll find that for each bushel (20.4 kg) of apples, 7 or 8 cups (1.7 to 1.9 l) of liquid will be required. Cover and cook over low heat. Stir frequently to prevent scorching and to allow for uniform cooking. When the apples are soft, you may pass them through a sieve or a food mill to remove any remaining seeds and uncooked skins. Return the apples to the pot and bring to a boil. Cook for 10 minutes or until the sauce reaches the desired consistency. Add sugar or spices as desired.

3.

While the apples are cooking, prepare your jars and canner (see "Water-Bath Canning" on the opposite page).

4.

Fill the jars with the applesauce to within 1/2" (1.3 cm) of their tops, and run a small rubber spatula around the inside surface of each jar to release any trapped air.

5.

Follow the instructions provided in Steps 6 through 10 of "Canning Apple Slices."

CANNING APPLE JUICE

For the best results, start with apple juice that has been pressed within 24 hours of beginning the canning process.

1.

Refrigerate the apple juice, leaving it undisturbed for 24 to 48 hours so that the sediment in it will settle.

2.

Ladle or siphon off the clean liquid, and discard the sediment.

CONTINUED ON PAGE 165

HOT-PACK PROCESSING TIMES IN PRESSURE CANNER

Note the adjusted times for processing at certain altitudes.

■ DIAL-GAUGE CANNER ■

Contents	Jar Size	Time	At Altitudes of 0 to 2,000' (0-610 m)	At Altitudes of 2,001' to 4,000' (610-1,219 m)
Sliced Apples	Pints or quarts (473 or .9 l)	8 minutes	6 pounds (2.7 kg)	7 pounds (3.2 kg)
Applesauce	Pints or quarts	8 minutes	6 pounds	7 pounds

■ WEIGHTED-GAUGE CANNER ■

Contents	Jar Size	Time	At Altitudes of 0 to 2,000' (0-610 m)	At Altitudes of 2,001' to 4,000' (610-1,219 m)
Sliced Apples	Pints or quarts	8 minutes	5 pounds (2.3 kg)	10 pounds (4.5 kg)
Applesauce	Pints or quarts	8 minutes	5 pounds	10 pounds

Apples IN THE *Pantry*

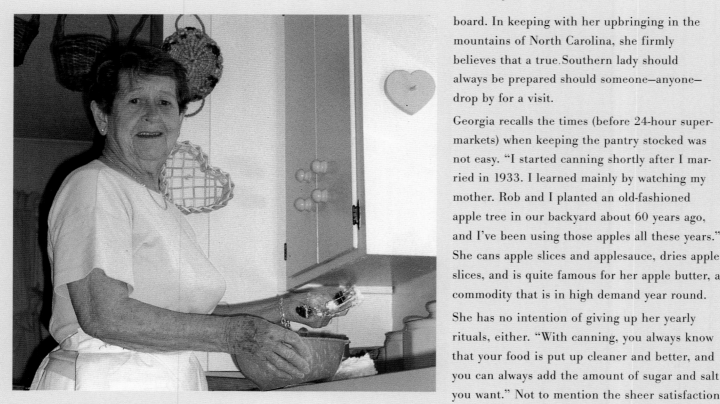

Eighty-two year old Georgia Shuford has spent the better part of her life making sure there's always something in the cupboard. In keeping with her upbringing in the mountains of North Carolina, she firmly believes that a true.Southern lady should always be prepared should someone—anyone—drop by for a visit.

Georgia recalls the times (before 24-hour supermarkets) when keeping the pantry stocked was not easy. "I started canning shortly after I married in 1933. I learned mainly by watching my mother. Rob and I planted an old-fashioned apple tree in our backyard about 60 years ago, and I've been using those apples all these years." She cans apple slices and applesauce, dries apple slices, and is quite famous for her apple butter, a commodity that is in high demand year round.

She has no intention of giving up her yearly rituals, either. "With canning, you always know that your food is put up cleaner and better, and you can always add the amount of sugar and salt you want." Not to mention the sheer satisfaction of pulling out a jar of homemade apple butter to eat with steaming biscuits in the company of dear old friends.

If desired, filter the juice through a paper coffee filter or a few layers of cheesecloth.

3.

Quickly bring the juice to a boil in a stainless steel or enameled pot.

4.

Proceed as outlined in "Canning Apple Slices," filling the sterile jars immediately and leaving 1/4" (6 mm) headroom at the top of each one. The juice should be processed in a boiling-water bath for 5 minutes.

PROCESSING IN A PRESSURE CANNER

Place a jar rack, 2" (5.1 cm) of water, and the sealed jars in the pressure canner. Fasten the lid securely, and set on high heat. After steam exhausts from the canner for 10 minutes, add the weighted gauge or close the petcock to pressurize the canner. Start timing the process when the desired pressure is reached. Adjust the heat to maintain a uniform pressure, and process the jars for the recommended times.

When processing is complete, remove the canner from the heat, and allow it to air-cool until it is fully depressurized. Slowly remove the weighted gauge or open the petcock, wait 2 more minutes, and carefully remove the canner lid. Remove the jars from the canner, and place on a towel or a rack.

FREEZING APPLES

If canning is out of the question, apple slices, applesauce, cider, and baked or unbaked pies may all be frozen.

FREEZING APPLE SLICES

Freezing apple slices inevitably softens them and causes some loss of flavor, but the preserved fruit is nevertheless suitable for cooking. The following instructions will provide you with about 4 quarts (3.8 l) of frozen apple slices. Note that no sugar is called for in these instructions. If you like, you can cover the fruit with a medium syrup or toss with 1/2 cup (100 g) sugar per quart (.9 l) of fruit, and freeze in sealed plastic containers instead.

1.

Wash, peel, core, and slice 12 medium apples (about 4 pounds or 1.8 kg). To prevent discoloration, drop the slices into a bowl containing 1 gallon (3.8 l) of water mixed with 2 tablespoons of lemon juice.

2.

Bring about 1 gallon (3.8 l) of water to a boil, and working in batches (about four should do it), drain the apples and drop them into the water. Cook for 1 minute, then scoop out, drain immediately, and arrange in single layers on cookie sheets. Continue until all the apples are done.

3.

Place the cookie sheets in the freezer. When the slices are completely frozen, pack in plastic freezer bags, seal, and return to the freezer.

FREEZING APPLESAUCE AND CIDER

Both applesauce and cider may be frozen. Allow the sauce to cool, and pack it in rigid plastic freezer containers with tight-fitting lids, leaving 1/2" (1.3 cm) of headroom for pints and 1" (2.5) for quarts. Label and freeze.

Although refrigerated cider will hold its flavor for one to two weeks, freezing is a better way to preserve it. Pack as you would applesauce.

FREEZING PIES

To freeze baked pies, first make sure the pie is completely cool. Wrap before placing in the freezer. To serve a baked, frozen pie, place in a preheated 375°F (190°C) oven for approximately 30 minutes. If the crust begins to brown too quickly, cover it with a loose piece of aluminum foil.

Unbaked pies freeze very well. Assemble the pies as usual, but don't cut any steam vents in the top crust before wrapping and freezing. When ready to bake, unwrap, cut the steam vents, and place the frozen pie in a preheated 425°F (218°C) oven for 30 minutes. Reduce the heat to 375°F (190°C), and continue baking for an additional 30 to 40 minutes. Cover the crust with aluminum foil if it gets too brown.

CIDER MILL   WILLIAM TOLMAN CARLTON
NEW YORK STATE HISTORICAL ASSOCIATION, COOPERSTOWN, NY

DRYING APPLES

Why would you want to dry apples? If you've got plenty of freezer space or you enjoy canning, you may not, but let me warn you that chewy, tart, and sweet apple slices can become an addictive snack. The slices may also be reconstituted and used in a wide variety of recipes.

Select tart, firm varieties for drying. Wash, peel, and core the apples, and slice them into rings or wedges about 1/4" (6 mm) thick. If you're using an electric dehydrator, arrange the slices in a single layer on each tray, and dry at 115°F (46°C) for about 8 hours. Turn the fruit once to encourage even air distribution.

If your heat source is the sun, first make drying trays by building simple wooden frames and stapling cheesecloth across them. Pretreat the sliced fruit by soaking it for an hour in a solution of lemon juice and water to prevent discoloration. Arrange the slices on the trays, cover with another layer of cheesecloth, and place in a well-ventilated location that gets full sun. (Elevate the trays so that air can circulated underneath them.) Turn the fruit every few hours so that all portions will be exposed. Bring the trays indoors as soon the sun sets, and take them out again in the morning. Three days of sun drying will yield delicious dried slices that are chewy, but not so leathery that you can't bite through them.

Oven-dried apple slices are also easy to make. Spread the slices on baking sheets, and dry for about 8 hours at 115°F (46°C), testing every hour or two until the slices have dried.

To reconstitute dried apples, just soak them in hot water or apple juice, with a little added lemon juice, until they have softened. This may take up to 3 hours. To make applesauce, drain the soaked fruit, add spices (see page 000), and purée in a blender, adding soaking liquid as necessary.

We all feel the demands placed by our modern world to go faster and to consume more. As a result, many of us feel separated from the rhythms of the natural world. If you believe, as Thomas Jefferson did, that "the soil is the gift of God to the living," planting, cultivating, and harvesting an apple orchard can be a way to reestablish a relationship with the earth.

It was JEFFERSON's vision that America would become a nation of small producers living on the land. The orchardists whom I have met—from Virginia to California and North Carolina to Michigan—lead lives in some ways similar to those Jefferson envisioned. Each is striving to preserve the rhythms and pleasures of a simpler way of life.

In the CRANE household, apples are a family tradition, one that started in 1916, when H.B. Crane purchased a farm near what was then Fenn's Mill, Michigan. Because the farm was located in a 100-mile stretch of land with prevailing winds from Lake Michigan, H.B. decided that a fruit crop would be ideal. Indeed, fruit prospered on the Crane farm and a fondness for fruit, particularly the beloved apple, has been in the family ever since.

What started out as a small farm is now a thriving business—the 300-acre Crane Orchards in Fennville, including a "U-pick orchard" (designed to "cut out the middle man"), a cider press,

a bed-and-breakfast, and a family restaurant called Crane's Pie Pantry Restaurant. Robert and Lue, the eldest Cranes, have the support (and labor) of all five children and two spouses. The entire operation is a family affair, with the sixth generation—the Crane's eighteen-year-old granddaughter, Mia—recently installed as innkeeper.

The orchard has been modernized over the years, but that doesn't mean the Cranes have lost their sense of nostalgia— quite the contrary. They beam with pride when they discuss their apple heritage.

TOM BURFORD, known to many as "Mr. Apple," lives in a special world. As this nurseryman shares his world in conversation, there's no doubt that its center is apples: growing them, selling them, and eating them. His speech is filled with apple-related stories—stories about a special jelly his aunt used to make, about a recipe for cider-curing a ham from an apple-fed pig, and about discovering some forgotten perry (a combination of pear and apple juice) his father had put up that turned out to be the best perry vinegar anyone had ever tasted. One can't help but feel that Tom's main purpose in life is to share the wonder of apples.

Tom's ancestors settled in the Amherst, Virginia area in 1817 and have been orchardists ever since. Monroe, Virginia, where Tom

ABOVE: TOM BURFORD

UPPER RIGHT: THE ORCHARDS AT WARREN WILSON COLLEGE

RIGHT: THOMAS JEFFERSON

lives, isn't far from the famous apple orchards at Thomas Jefferson's residence, Monticello. Tom claims that his goal isn't so much to preserve old apple varieties as it is to educate people about apple varieties and their heritage. Whether he spends his time trying to find the lost Jefferson variety, Taliaferro (known to Virginians as Tolliver) or introducing new cultivars with their own special character, Tom's focus in life is the fruit he loves so much.

At Warren Wilson College in Swannanoa, North Carolina, IAN ROBERTSON preserves the English methods of cider making, teaching his students the secrets of making *scrumpy* (or young cider.)

Like Tom Burford, JESSE SCHWARTZ, in Berkeley, California, is working hard to preserve disappearing apple varieties. Jesse has also established The Living Tree community, which incorporates the preservation, propagation, and care of trees as a spiritual directive.

We owe these men and women (and the thousands of orchardists they represent) a huge debt of gratitude for the choices they have made. Without their dedication to apples, in orchards large and small, we might never know the succulent tastes and special pleasures that different apple varieties can provide.

LEFT: ANTIQUE DELIVERY TRUCK AT THE CRANE ORCHARDS

TOP: TURN-OF-THE-CENTURY APPLE PICKERS AT THE CRANE ORCHARDS

ABOVE LEFT: DWIGHT CRANE, WHO SETTLED IN FENNVILLE AROUND 1870

ABOVE RIGHT: LYDIA CRANE, WIFE OF DWIGHT

This book was born during a street-corner conversation with an old friend, ROB PULLEYN, who now happens to be my publisher. As the pages were created, my appreciation deepened for all the minds and hands that made it possible. The writing grew better because my editor knew how to clarify my ideas, the food grew better because the photographer understood how to shoot it, and the content grew better because so many people were willing to share their knowledge and insights with me. To all of the people listed below, thanks.

—IAN ROBERTSON (Director of the Work Program Office), DONNA PRICE (Garden Manager), and IAN'S STUDENTS at Warren Wilson College (Swannanoa, NC), who provided a great afternoon of cider making and a funny moment as we dumped several tons of apples in the wrong place. Many of the photos in this book were taken at the Warren Wilson orchards.

—The DEVELOPMENT AND PUBLIC AFFAIRS OFFICE at MONTICELLO (Charlottesville, VA) and the THOMAS JEFFERSON MEMORIAL FOUNDATION for providing photographer Evan Bracken and myself with a tour of Thomas Jefferson's home and for having invited us to attend an apple-tasting event held at Monticello. The Foundation's support was invaluable to us.

—DR. RICK UNRATH and J.D. OBERMILLER from the North Carolina Agricultural Experimental Station (Fletcher, NC) for so generously sharing their knowledge

—PETER HATCH (Monticello, Charlottesville, VA) and TOM BURFORD (Burford Brothers, Monroe, VA), who taught me about the two different types of orchards in our early history: the "gentleman's" orchard and the seedling orchard. Peter helped me understand that technological, chemical, biological, and mechanical interventions make modern orchards possible.

—TEX HARRISON (owner of Complements to the Chef, Asheville, NC), who virtually emptied her wonderful shop of its many beautiful dishes and serving pieces as we used them during photography sessions

—JAMIE and ELSPETH McCLURE CLARKE, and their daughter ANNIE AGER, who allowed us to have our harvest picnic in their orchards (see pages 148-49). Their family-owned roadside business, Hickory Nut Gap Farm (Route 74-A, Fairview, NC), specializes in fresh apples and apple cider and is open from Labor Day until November 1 each year.

—JESSE SCHWARTZ, of the Living Tree Community (Berkeley, CA), a community leader whose orchards serve as a spiritual focal point

—SHANNA DUNCAN of the INTERNATIONAL APPLE INSTITUTE in McLean, VA, for having permitted us to reproduce her article on apple-eating styles. The article, with minor changes, appears on page 19 and has been retitled "A Matter of Style."

—LAURA FOSTER NICHOLSON (Chicago, IL), the extraordinary textile artist who, at our request, created the brocaded weavings shown on pages 85 and 109

—SKYTOP ORCHARD in Hendersonville, NC, and KAY HIPPS, also of Hendersonville, for their help with location photography

—My editor, CHRIS RICH (Lark Books, Asheville, NC), who helped me organize myself, did much of my worrying for me, and kept me going in the right direction

—Photographer EVAN BRACKEN (Light Reflections, Hendersonville, NC), whose skill helped me succeed where many cooks fail—in helping readers to dine with their eyes. Of course, Evan was well fed while we worked, but it was a pleasure to cook for him. His appreciation kept me inspired.

—Art director DANA IRWIN (Lark Books, Asheville, NC), whose keen eye has helped this book tell wonderful visual stories and whose willingness to collect materials as she traveled was very much appreciated

—GEORGIA SHUFORD (Marion, North Carolina), expert apple canner and grandmother of assistant editor Laura Dover, for having so graciously helped us with location photography

—A final, special thanks is due to publisher ROB PULLEYN. He knows I can cook, but committing himself to this book was an act of faith. Without his support, this project would never have happened.

The editor would like to thank assistant editor LAURA DOVER (Lark Books, Asheville, NC), whose inspired and steadfast help and friendship make being an editor possible. Thanks also to ELAINE THOMPSON at Lark Books for her patience under duress.

ADDITIONAL PHOTOGRAPHY

The photographs that appear on the pages listed in this section were graciously contributed courtesy of the following individuals and organizations:

The **Crane** family (Crane Orchards, Fennville, MI) and **Dana Irwin** (Lark Books, Asheville, NC)

—back cover (second from top) and pages 5 (bottom left), 67, 73, 113, 115, 125, 144, and 169

The **New York State Historical Association** (Cooperstown, NY)

—page 5 (top): *Apple Picking*; artist unidentified; oil on canvas; 25" x 30"; N-439.61

—page 36: *Music and Refreshments* by George Cochran Lambdin (1830-1896); oil on canvas; 1875, 22" x 29"; N-414.55

—page 155: *Cider Making on Long Island* by William M. Davis (1829-1920); oil on canvas; ca. 1870, 17" x 28-3/4"; N-368.55

—page 165: *Cider Mill* by William Tolman Carlton (1816-1888); oil on canvas; ca. 1855, 32" x 26-1/4"; N-427.55

The **New Zealand Apple & Pear Marketing Board** (Hastings, New Zealand) and **Christine McRae**

—The photos of Braeburn, Fuji, Royal Gala, Granny Smith, and Red Delicious apples in the chart that begins on page 8

—page 5 (bottom right)

Marvin A. Owings, Jr., agricultural extension agent and pomologist (North Carolina Cooperative Extension Service, Hendersonville, NC)

—pages 27, 35, 39, 53, 55, 65, 79, 83, 89, 117, 139 (bottom), 142 (left), 145, and 147

Cheryl Richter of Richter, Ryman & Co., Marketing (Lincoln, NE)

—page 136 (top) © 1995

Washington State Apple Commission (Wenatchee, WA)

—The photos of Criterion, Gala, Golden Delicious, Jonagold, Newtown Pippin, Rome Beauty, and Winesap apples in the chart that begins on page 8

—front cover, inside front cover, and pages 3, 29, 41, 75, 119, 127, and 129

RELATED TITLES
Candy!

A Sweet Selection of Fun & Easy Recipes
By Laura Dover Doran
$24.95 ($36.95 Can.) Hardcover with concealed wire binding, 128 pages, 130 color photos ISBN 1-57990-055-0
$9.95 Paperback (special) ISBN 1-57990-111-5

ANTIQUE APPLE: *an old variety, usually discovered in the wild as opposed to having been bred*

APPLE BRANDY: *the final product of fermenting and distilling fresh apple cider*

APPLEJACK: *a form of apple brandy distilled from hard cider. Traditionally made by freezing. Also known as frozen heart*

APPLE JUICE: *the filtered, unfermented, and pasteurized juice from apples*

BLOOM PERIOD: *the period of flowering when a blossom is receptive to pollination*

CENTRAL LEADER: *a method of training and pruning apple trees which entails the selection of one central, upright shoot, with one zone of shoots to form the first whorl of laterals*

CIDER APPLE: *an apple with a good balance of sugar, acid, and tannin. Makes a flavorful juice when pressed*

CLONE: *a tree propagated by grafting. The offspring is identical to the parent. Clones, as opposed to seedlings, do not reflect genetic variation.*

CORDON: *a method of training and pruning best suited for small, domestic orchards. Trees are normally planted and grown at an angle and limited to a single stem, with all laterals pruned back in the summer.*

CRAB APPLE: *a small, very tart apple. Believed to be the progenitor of modern apples*

DESSERT APPLE: *an apple best suited for eating fresh (or "out of hand")*

DWARF TREE: *a tree grown on rootstock that limits its final height to 6' to 8' (1.8 to 2.4 m) or 35 percent of standard height*

ESPALIER: *a method of training and pruning in which branches are trained horizontally in a single plane, usually against a wall or fence*

GRAFTING: *a method of propagation in which two different plants are joined in order to take advantage of special characteristics of each*

GREENING: *any apple that is green when it is mature (e.g. Rhode Island Greening)*

HALF STANDARD TREE: *a tree grown on rootstock that limits tree height to half the standard height, about 20' (6.1 m)*

HIGH DENSITY ORCHARD: *an orchard planted with dwarf trees and managed intensively. Usually contains 300 to 900 trees per acre (4047 square m)*

INTERSTEM: *a grafting method in which rootstock and scion are joined by an intermediate graft*

LATERALS: *horizontal branches*

LOW DENSITY ORCHARD: *an orchard planted with standard or half-standard trees, spaced traditionally with 40 to 60 trees per acre (4047 square m)*

PEARMAIN: *a loose grouping of apple varieties that are pear-like in shape or flavor*

pH: *a measure of acidity or alkalinity. A pH of 7 indicates a neutral balance. Ranges from ph 1 to ph 7 are acidic, and ranges from pH 7 to pH 14 are alkaline.*

PIPPIN: *an apple raised from a seed*

PRUNING: *a method of trimming trees to control growth and promote health*

REINETTE: *an apple with a spotted appearance*

ROOTSTOCK: *the term used in grafting to describe the root system*

RUSSET: *an apple with a rough, mottled skin*

SCION: *the term used in grafting to describe the upper portion of the graft; the fruiting portion*

SEEDLING: *a tree grown from a seed*

SEMI-DWARF: *a tree grown on rootstock that limits its final height to 50 percent of standard height, or 9' to 15' (2.7 to 4.6 m)*

SOIL TEST: *a method of determining the chemical balance and fertility of soil*

SPORT: *a genetic variation on a part of a tree, such as a limb that produces an apple different in color from the others on the tree*

STANDARD TREE: *a tree grown on its own rootstock or on a rootstock that allows the tree to reach its natural height, usually up to 40' (12.2 m)*

STRAIN: *a variation within a specific variety*

TWO-PART GRAFT: *a method of grafting together a rootstock and a scion*

VARIETY: *a variation on a species*

VINTAGE CIDER APPLE: *an apple that will make good cider without having to be blended with other apple varieties*

BEIGNETS: *light, deep-fried, risen cakes. Similar to doughnuts*

BLANCHING: *the process of rapidly immersing in boiling water, usually to cook a fruit or vegetable lightly or to assist in peeling its skin*

CALVADOS: *a distinctive apple brandy, made in Calvados*

CANAPÉ: *appetizer; small hors-d'oeuvre*

CAPON: *fattened, neutered rooster*

CAUL FAT: *the thin layer of fat, lacy in appearance, that forms around the intestines of cows, sheep, and pigs. Used in cooking to hold rolled and stuffed items together when roasted or sautéed*

CHIFFONADE: *cut into thin ribbons*

CHUTNEY: *a spicy fruit condiment, frequently made with ginger and molasses*

CIDER, FRESH: *the just-pressed, unfermented juice of apples*

CIDER, HARD: *the fermented juice of apples*

COUNTRY HAM: *a dried and salt-cured ham. Must be washed and soaked before using*

COUSCOUS: *a grain frequently used in Middle Eastern cooking*

CRÈME FRAÎCHE: *a cross between fresh heavy cream and sour cream*

ESCALOPE: *a butchery method, in which a piece of meat, poultry, or fish is sliced and then pounded until thin*

FORCEMEAT: *a stuffing, often with a sausage-like composition*

FREE-RANGE CHICKEN: *a chicken allowed to roam and graze freely. Usually raised without administration of antibiotics or other growth stimulants*

FRITTER: *a small mass of fried or sautéed batter made with corn meal or flour and eggs, often containing fruit or meat within. Related to pancakes and doughnuts, but the batter is thicker as it must adhere to the food being fried*

GANACHE: *a mixture of chocolate and heavy cream, used as a filling or as a base for other chocolate concoctions, such as chocolate truffles*

GOZA WRAPPER: *a round, flour wrapper used in Oriental cooking. Similar to a wonton wrapper, which is square*

GRATIN: *any dish that is baked (usually with cream) and then finished under the broiler to produce a browned top*

JULIENNE: *Cut into strips shaped like matchsticks*

LEMON ZEST: *a fine scraping of the outer rind of a lemon. Does not include the bitter white portion*

NEAT: *to serve a drink without any garnish or ice*

PANCETTA: *the same cut of meat as bacon, salted instead of smoked, and generally found in a rolled-up form. Salt pork makes an adequate substitute.*

PAPILLOTE (EN PAPILLOTE): *to cook in a sealed paper package or bag*

PAUPIETTE: *a little "package." In cooking, a thin escalope of meat or poultry that is stuffed, rolled, and braised*

PHYLLO DOUGH: *a very thin pastry, made by stretching the dough. Used for strudels and other "wrapped" foods*

POACH: *to cook by immersing the food in a simmering liquid such as water or stock*

POLENTA: *the Italian name for corn meal and for the method of cooking it to produce a creamy textured "mush." Known in the southern United States as grits*

PURÉE: *to cook or process until the texture is like very thick cream or applesauce*

RAGOÛT: *a dish similar to stew*

RAISED: *Leavened with yeast, baking soda, baking powder, or whipped egg whites*

RATATOUILLE: *usually an eggplant and tomato dish, made by browning and then simmering the ingredients*

REDUCE: *to concentrate flavor and thicken by removing much of the water content*

RENDER: *to cause a food to release its liquid or fat by cooking over low heat*

ROULADE: *a "roll." A jelly roll is a roulade made with a sponge cake.*

SAUTÉ: *French for "to make jump." Cooking in a flat, open skillet or sauté pan over high heat, usually with fat, to produce a crispy, brown exterior*

SIMPLE SYRUP: *A boiled combination of sugar and water. Used in confectionery and in the making of frozen fruit sorbets (sherbets)*

SORBET: *a frozen dessert. An ice or sherbet which can be made with or without cream or egg whites. The simplest form is a combination of simple syrup and fruit juice.*

SOUFFLÉ: *a baked dish that gains height and lightness from the addition of beaten egg whites. Soufflés are usually served as a first or last dish, as they fall quickly and easily.*

SWEAT: *To cause a food to release some of its moisture by applying low heat. (Rendering is similar, but usually releases all the liquid.)*

TEMPER: *to gently raise or lower the temperature of a food. Chocolate is tempered from its melting point to a temperature slightly higher than that at which it resolidifies.*

TIMBALE: *a small, cylindrical mold, the closed end of which is smaller than the open end. Used for cooking light purées that are often held together and set with eggs. A dish cooked in one of these molds is usually called a "timbale of — ."*

TISANE: *a beverage consisting of a light infusion, traditionally consumed to promote health or dispel illness*

TRUFFLE: *a wild, usually round fungus with a unique earthy flavor. Very rare and expensive. Hunted with the help of trained dogs or pigs. Also, a chocolate made in the shape of this fungus*

VERJUS: *in the purest sense, a very tart, acidic juice made from unripe apples or grapes. In modern versions, tart juice and alcohol are combined and aged with vinegar.*

METRIC CONVERSION CHARTS

LINEAR

Inches	CM	Inches	CM	Inches	CM	Inches	CM
1/8	0.3	4-1/2	11.4	20	50.8	36	91.4
1/4	0.6	5	12.7	21	53.3	37	94.0
3/8	1.0	6	15.2	22	55.9	38	96.5
1/2	1.3	7	17.8	23	58.4	39	99.1
5/8	1.6	8	20.3	24	61.0	40	101.6
3/4	1.9	9	22.9	25	63.5	41	104.1
7/8	2.2	10	25.4	26	66.0	42	106.7
1	2.5	11	27.9	27	68.6	43	109.2
1-1/4	3.2	12	30.5	28	71.1	44	111.8
1-1/2	3.8	13	33.0	29	73.7	45	114.3
1-3/4	4.4	14	35.6	30	76.2	46	116.8
2	5.1	15	38.1	31	78.7	47	119.4
2-1/2	.4	16	40.6	32	81.3	48	121.9
3	7.6	17	43.2	33	83.8	49	124.5
3-1/2	8.9	18	45.7	34	86.4	50	127.0
4	10.2	19	48.3	35	88.9		